Shakespearean Design

Shakespearean Design

Mark Rose

The
Belknap
Press
of
Harvard
University
Press

Cambridge
Massachusetts

To Rose and Sydney Rose

Preface

This book is a study of Renaissance dramaturgy—that is, a discussion of some of the general principles according to which Shakespeare's plays are constructed. Shakespeare has been studied and written about for so many hundreds of years that it must appear foolish to suppose there can be anything very novel left to say about him. Shakespeareans tend to be suspicious—and rightly so—of claims to novelty. Anything that is very "original" in this field is likely to be merely perverse. Lively perversity may sometimes have value in the continuing dialogue about Shakespeare; most often, however, it muddies the waters, stirring up controversies that are a waste of time and energy.

Let me emphasize, then, that my own approach to Shakespearean structure, while it may be different from some, is by no means radically original. Despite the misleading act divisions, sensitive critics have always been more or less aware of the general organization of the plays. Bradley, for instance, who does not question the idea of five acts, nevertheless in practice often thinks of the plays in terms of two movements with a crisis located in the middle. Others have compared Shakespearean structure to an arch with the turning point in the plot as the keystone, or have spoken of a central climatic plateau.[1] I believe that much of what I say in

1. See "Construction in Shakespeare's Tragedies," in *Shakespearean Tragedy,* 2nd ed. (London: Macmillan, 1905), pp. 40–8. The metaphor of the arch is Richard G. Moulton's. His quaintly "scientific" *Shakespeare as a Dramatic Artist,* originally published in 1885, is not much read today, but is interesting nevertheless. Unlike most critics of his age, Moulton has a spatial sensibility, but he has little idea of any aspects of structure other than character and plot and no idea of the function of the scene as a unit. Bernard Beckerman develops the idea of the climactic plateau in his excellent chapter on dramaturgy in *Shakespeare at the Globe 1599–1609* (New York: Macmillan, 1962), pp. 24–62.

this book will simply be making explicit things that many readers have felt, if somewhat vaguely. Nevertheless, I hope that the total effect will be to influence the way we look at the plays, sharpening our sense of them as specifically Renaissance artifacts, and giving us new tools for use in the classroom as well as in the study.

The particular aspect of Shakespearean structure with which I am concerned I call "design." Rather than define the term now, I shall allow it to remain flexible, trusting that what I mean by it will emerge as the discussion progresses. Indeed, the whole matter of terminology is a problem, for whereas we have a well-developed language for talking about the structure of classical drama, we have nothing equivalent for Shakespearean drama. Practically the only term of any help at all is "scene," a word that is used so variously in Shakespeare criticism that it sometimes seems to be synonymous with "episode" or even "speech." A critic attempting to talk concretely about Shakespearean structure has two choices. He can either create an artificial language of his own, which has the advantage of precision; or he can make do with whatever words seem most useful at each stage in the argument, which has the advantage of comprehensibility. In general, I have chosen the latter course.

The little charts and diagrams may initially give a false impression. I included these charts only reluctantly, deciding that, inelegant as they are, they provide an economical way of making certain matters clear. The numbers, usually line totals, sprinkled throughout may also give a false impression of exactness. I indicate line totals usually only to give a rough idea of the general proportions of a particular scene or segment. The edition I use is Alfred Harbage's *Complete Pelican Shakespeare* (Baltimore: Penguin Books, 1969), which, for reasons indicated in the first chapter, is the best text available for anyone interested in structure. Naturally the line totals will be slightly different in other editions, but the proportions will be much the same.

Given the nature of Shakespeare's art, it is impossible to separate structure and meaning. My primary interest, however, is not in offering new readings of the plays but in describing the way they are organized. Wherever possible I have tried to be uncontroversial in matters of interpretation, employing readings that will not divert attention from the main point. Most of my readings are, I hope, the common property of all Shakespeareans, and I have only occasionally annotated interpretative points. To those whose critical insights I may have borrowed without giving due credit, my thanks and apologies.

This short book might easily have been triple its length, but I have not sought to be comprehensive or complete—only, I hope, suggestive. Not every play of Shakespeare's is discussed or even mentioned. In particular I have slighted the comedies in favor of the histories and tragedies, which are, from ny point of view, more interesting. In selecting examples to illustrate my points I have tried in principle to choose from Shakespeare's best-known plays.

Differently conceived, this book might have taken the form of a survey of all Elizabethan drama, in which case it might have been ten times its length. I have not reconsidered all of Elizabethan drama in the light of this study, but I have sunk enough trial shafts to be able to suggest a few tentative conclusions. Shakespeare's principles of design are not unique. Many of his predecessors, especially those who wrote for the professional troupes and public theaters, appear to use similar principles of design. Even such an early and relatively crude play as *Cambises* reveals conscious design in the internal organization of scenes. Marlowe's plays are particularly ,nteresting in connection with Shakespeare's. Individual scenes in Marlowe often compare favorably in design with scenes in early Shakespeare. But, so far as I can tell, no one before Shakespeare appears to have been sufficiently in control of the overall structure of his plays to apply the principles of scene design to the play as a whole. (It is just possible, however, that Marlowe was feeling his way toward an overall design in *Edward II.*) Shakespeare's influence can be traced in later writers such as Webster and Tourneur. *The White Devil,* for example, is designed on much the same pattern as *Hamlet* or *Lear,* Vittoria's trial coming in approximately the middle and forming a great emblematic centerpiece for the play as a whole. In *The Revenger's Tragedy,* usually attributed to Tourneur, the centerpiece is Vindice's murder of the duke, the long scene in which he tricks the duke into kissing Gloriana's poisoned skull. None of the plays, however, shows anything quite like Shakespeare's masterly control of his art: in design, as in so many other matters, Shakespeare is beyond the reach of all his rivals. The one playwright with a sense of structure that approaches Shakespeare's is Jonson. But Jonson is self-consciously "classical." His act divisions do appear to have significance, and, structurally, his plays are more closely related to the developing neoclassical drama than to the Shakespearean form of design.

The book begins with a discussion of certain critical and historical matters such as the conception of the sister arts, poetry and painting, ideas of spatial form, and the importance of proportion in Renaissance aesthetics. The second chapter analyzes the internal organization of a few representative scenes. (So far as I know there has never been an extended study of the internal organization of Shakespeare's scenes, although many scholars have recognized the importance of the cleared-stage scene as his basic structural unit and the need for such a study. My chapter obviously does not fill that need, but I hope it indicates some interesting directions for inquiry to pursue.)[2] The third chapter discusses some of the ways scenes are related to each other. I try to minimize the space devoted to points already well understood, such as Shakespeare's use of ironic juxtaposition, focusing on less familiar matters—structural echoes between scenes, the use of formal thematic liaisons, and the function of the designed group of scenes as a structural unit. The *Hamlet* chapter provides a scene-by-scene structural analysis of a representative play, attempting to suggest, among other things, the practical value of

2. These words were written before the appearance of Emrys Jones *Scenic Form in Shakespeare* (Oxford: Oxford University Press, 1971), which contains some interesting analyses of scenes and suggests that Shakespeare often used his own earlier work as "sources" for scenes in later plays. Jones's approach to structure is quite different from my own; nevertheless, in places he implicitly confirms my sense of the spatial form of various scenes.

the scenic approach in the classroom. This section may be regarded as the pivot between the earlier discussions of component units and the last two chapters, which deal with overall design. These final chapters are organized more or less chronologically, the fifth treating selected plays from the 1590's, the sixth beginning with *Julius Caesar* and discussing the great tragedies, *Antony and Cleopatra,* and the late romances. In these two chapters I have tried simultaneously to present representative examples of Shakespearean design and to indicate, at least in outline, something of the way this aspect of his art develops during his career. In the discussion of one play—*Romeo and Juliet,* in which the relationship between Shakespeare's tragedy and Arthur Brooke's poem presents relatively few scholarly problems—I have tried to suggest how examination of design casts some light on the way Shakespeare reworks his sources.

My thanks are due to Yale University for a Morse Fellowship which allowed me a year's leave of absence to complete this book. I am also indebted to the many colleagues at Yale who listened with patience and offered encouragement and useful advice at every stage of my work. Years ago I was fortunate enough to study with Alfred Harbage at Harvard, and it was in his seminars that the germ of this book, the idea of examining the internal organization of scenes, originated. For many years, too, I have been engaged in vigorous discussion of Shakespeare with Howard Felperin, and without our conversations my understanding of the plays would be immeasurably poorer. Phyllis Rose read and commented on the entire manuscript and helped considerably in the shaping of the final work.

Contents

Contexts of Design

Approaches to Structure

That Shakespeare's plays are not like modern drama, even modern poetic drama, is well known. We all realize the special qualities of the Elizabethan stage, that ornamented but unlocalized platform which permitted the playwrights such marvelous flexibility. But Shakespeare is not a modern man in disguise, a Connecticut Yankee at Queen Elizabeth's court, graciously complying with a few old conventions about locale, disguise, character types, plot types, and such. He is to the core a man of his time, and he is profoundly different from ourselves. Knowledge of the physical capabilities of the Elizabethan stage is essential to an understanding of Shakespeare's dramaturgy, but this alone has taken us only so far. The principles that give order and meaning to the plays spring from deeper sources: they have to do with the very shape of Renaissance thought.

Most of us in reading or seeing Shakespeare probably come away with relatively little sense of structure. We have a strong sense of character and of incident, striking moments like Hamlet in the graveyard, Lear in the storm, or Lady Macbeth scrubbing her hands, and a somewhat vaguer sense of the general thrust of the action. We probably recollect also something of the mood of various episodes, the lyric joy of the balcony scene in *Romeo and Juliet* or the ominous sultriness that descends upon the stage before the duels in which Mercutio and Tybalt are slain. Particular phrases, lines, and speeches of course remain with us, and so do image patterns, certainly the more obvious ones such as the opposition of darkness and light in *Othello,* and, perhaps, since we have been trained in this way of thinking, the more subtle ones too, such as the clothing imagery in *Macbeth.* Depending upon taste and training, some of us will also come away with a strong sense of such matters as ritualistic action or the archetypal patterns that are, in a broad sense, "structure." In the more limited and usual sense of the term, however, we do not generally perceive much "structure" in Shakespeare. The plays probably seem to most of us magnificent but loose, the brilliant if rather shapeless—sometimes we say "organic"—flow of a great poetic mind working at white heat. In other words, they probably seem to us in organization not entirely unlike certain romantic poems, "Kubla Khan" perhaps, or Keats' odes.

Our anachronistic assumptions about Shakespearean structure are the inevitable result of the modern, "new critical," approach to Shakespeare. The critical orthodoxy of today, deriving largely from G. Wilson Knight's seminal work, maintains that the basic organization of the plays is poetic—that it is the patterns of imagery that inform the plays and give them meaning. Muriel Bradbrook, for example, has this to say: "The essential structure of Elizabethan drama lies not in the narrative or the characters but in the words. The greatest poets are also the greatest dramatists. Through their unique interest in word play and word patterns of all kinds the Elizabethans were especially fitted to build their drama on words."[1] This view, which has led to so much valuable analysis of imagery and rhetoric, clearly has much to recommend it, and yet it takes relatively little account of either the fact that Shakespeare is writing for the stage or that he is generally interested in telling a good story.

An older but still vital school of critics concentrates on pre cisely the area most modern writers deemphasize—dramatic narrative. The seminal work for this school is A. C. Bradley's lecture, "Construction in Shakespeare's Tragedies." Bradley is better known for character analysis, but in this lecture he applies a neo-Aristotelian method of plot analysis to Shakespeare, discussing the plays in terms of such matters as exposition, development, crisis, and catastrophe. More recently, Madeleine Doran has attempted to put the Elizabethan conception of plot into historical perspective, demonstrating through a survey of Renaissance aesthetic assumptions that the Elizabethan idea of form, of unity of action, was not the same as the classical idea. Miss Doran introduces the analogy of the visual arts and Heinrich Wölfflin's conception of "multiple unity"—that is, a composition in which the separate parts retain their independence even while they are related to the whole—as one of the defining characteristics of sixteenth-century art. This idea she uses to explain the episodic nature of Shakespeare's plots.[2]

Miss Doran's work seems to me very much on the right track; nevertheless she, like Bradley, remains more or less on the level of plot in her approach. If the limitation of the poetic school is that it tends to have difficulty distinguishing between a play and a lyric poem, the limitation of pure plot analysis—especially as practiced by Bradley—is that it tends to have difficulty distinguishing between poetic and prosaic drama, between Shakespeare and Scribe. Moreover, it fails to take account of the special nature of the Tudor dramatic tradition. Shakespeare has proved such a wonderful subject for interpretation, for analysis of images and themes and their relation to meaning, not only because his drama is in every sense poetic, but also because, emerging from the popular dramatic tradition of morality plays and interludes, he is himself as concerned with meaning as any critic. The popular drama of early Tudor England, which produced plays with titles like *All for Money* or *Enough Is as Good as a Feast,* was not so much a narrative art as a drama of ideas, a conceptual art. This is not to say that these plays do not tell stories—they do. But the structure of the stories, like the allegorical characters who enact them, is largely determined by idea: Everyman meets Death not simply because such an encounter has narrative interest but because it has theological significance. Even when the emphasis shifts and falls more heavily on narrative for its own sake, on the retelling of "histories" such as *Horestes* and *Cambises,* the conceptual element persists. The "naturalistic" characters still walk in a world partially populated by abstractions such as Truth, Duty, or Fame; but, more important, the "naturalistic" characters themselves are generally exemplary in conception—that is, they are presented to illustrate ideas, to provide examples of virtue or vice in action. The itinerant professional troupes that performed plays like *All for Money* or *Cambises* were the immediate ancestors of Shakespeare's own company, and the tradition of drama they created had, as we have more and more begun to realize in recent years, a profound effect on Shakespeare's own plays.[3]

A Shakespearean tragedy is not a morality play—"meaning" in Shakespeare is not something that can be summed up in a phrase or two—but then neither is it a *pièce-bien-faite,* simply a well-told story. Given the didactic dramatic tradition of Tudor England—and this is but a part of the larger didactic tradition of Elizabethan literary culture in general—analysis of Shakespearean structure merely in terms of narrative organization can be only partially successful. Ultimately, plot analysis alone does not speak directly to our sense of what the plays are about, what is important in them. Perhaps this is one reason why, compared to the poetic school, the narrative school of structure has been relatively uninfluential in the past forty years or so.

One immediate difficulty with a purely narrative approach is that it must stumble upon what Hereward T. Price calls "mirror-scenes," those very frequent episodes, such as the conversation of the gardeners in *Richard II,* the porter episode in *Macbeth,* or even the graveyard scene in *Hamlet,* which in no way advance the plot and often, too, contribute little to the dramatic excitement or to our understanding of the psychology of the major characters. Bradley does in fact stumble here, taking Shakespeare to task for "excessive development of matter neither required by the plot nor essential to the exhibition of character." Picking out Hamlet's speech to the players, he remarks that it seems to bring us close to Shakespeare himself, "but who can defend it from the point of view of constructive art?"[1] We are no longer inclined to see such episodes as faults, and a more adequate view of Shakespearean dramaturgy must be able to do precisely what Bradley assumed was impossible—explain the structural function of the speech to the players.

Hereward Price has given us a good start. Mirror-scenes, he points out, exist principally to reflect issues and themes rather than to advance the action. In them, Shakespeare concentrates upon creating symbols in order to shed light upon his central thought. Moreover, Price argues, the mirror-scenes provide a clue to the basic principle of the plays: "When Shakespeare adds one such scene to another, his principle of construction becomes clear. Meaning is all important to him."[5] Or, as he puts it elsewhere, the essence of Shakespearean dramaturgy is severely controlled "design," the relating of everything to the idea that constructs the play. Speaking in particular of the history plays, he says, "Critics who cannot follow Shakespeare's intentions pick holes in the construction of these plays. Looking for plot, they ignore design. It never occurs to them that Shakespeare was daringly original, that his mastery of design was just as superb as his mastery of language, and that his conception of design opens for modern times a new era in drama."[6]

Shakespeare's mastery of construction is indeed superb, but I am not certain that this aspect of his conception of structure, which has much in common with the morality tradition, is quite so daringly original as Price claims. In any case, the importance of Price's work is his recognition that Shakespearean structure cannot be defined in terms of narrative alone. Maynard Mack, in his "modest supplement" to Bradley's lecture, "The Jacobean Shakespeare," moves in the same direction as Price, if somewhat less dogmatically. After noting that Bradley's analysis is still the best description we have of the "outward shape" of Shakespearean tragedy, Mack remarks: "Still, it is impossible not to feel that Bradley missed something—that there is another kind of construction in Shakespeare's tragedies than the one he designates, more inward, more difficult to define, but not less significant. This other structure is not, like his, generated entirely by

5

the interplay of plot and character. Nor is it, on the other hand, though it is fashionable nowadays to suppose so, ultimately a verbal matter. It is poetic, but it goes well beyond what in certain quarters today is called (with something like a lump in the throat) 'the poetry.'" The "more inward" structure that Mack explores has to do with the suggestiveness of the relations between elements in the play, the way one kind of "voice" is played off against another, the way various kinds of "mirroring"—Mack uses the same term as Price—such as the repetition of the poisoning motif in *Hamlet*, establish significant connections between episodes, the way particular tableaux, exits, and entrances develop emblematic significance. He notes, for example, that in *Richard II*, the death of Gaunt, who takes a sacramental view of kingship and nation, comes at the instant Richard has destroyed the kind of society that makes such a view possible to maintain: Gaunt's death becomes an emblem for a larger death. Or, for another example, Mack notes that in the first scene of *Lear* it is significant that the king exits with Burgundy, the man who like himself has put externals first.[7]

Gaunt's death does not come where it does in the story merely for narrative or historical reasons, nor does Lear exit with Burgundy simply for dramatic convenience. Like Price's mirror-scenes, many of the aspects of dramaturgy that Mack discusses remind us of the morality tradition in which action is determined by idea. Tableaux, mirror-scenes, emblematic entrances and exits—all of these remind us, too, not only of what Mack calls Shakespeare's "visualizing imagination" but of the emblematic quality of Elizabethan thought in general, the pronounced tendency to think in concrete visual correlatives for abstract ideas or psychological realities: gardens for commonwealths, Fortune and her wheel for the vicissitudes of life, Cupid and his arrows for the passion of love. The sensibility that engendered the morality tradition is not wholly different from that which created *The Faerie Queene*, which is nevertheless so rich and sophisticated. Nor is Spenser's sensibility so very different from Shakespeare's as may, even today, sometimes be assumed.

Ut pictura poesis

The remarkable proliferation of emblem books in the six-teenth and seventeenth centuries is one of the most revealing phenomena of Renaissance culture, a clue to the visual, pictorial, sensibility of the age. The general influence—if "influence" is the right word for something so fundamental—of the emblem-atic mode of thought on writers such as Spenser and Shakespeare can now be taken for granted.[3] More interesting, however, than combing the emblem books for analogues to specific Shake-spearean images is to note how frequently those striking mo-ments that remain in our minds when the play is done—Hamlet in the graveyard, Lear in the storm, Lady Macbeth scrubbing her hands—possess a generally emblematic quality. I do not mean, of course, that we could ever adequately capture the graveyard scene by making a little woodcut of Hamlet with Yorick's skull in his hand, tacking on a *memento mori* poem to explain the picture. Yet part of the reason a moment like this remains with us is its significant resonance: it is not merely striking but mean-ingful as well.

Another clue to the special sensibility of the Renaissance is the pervasive idea of the "sister arts," poetry and painting, which we usually encounter under the rubric of the famous simile from Horace, *ut pictura poesis* ("as is painting so is poetry"), or in connection with the saying attributed to Simonides that painting is mute poetry, poetry a speaking picture. The popularity of the emblem books—collections of "speaking pictures"—is in fact part of this larger phenomenon in which the Renaissance tended to fuse the two arts into one. So close was the association that it was usual to assume correspondences between painting and po-etry in technique—between, say, the painter's use of color and the poet's use of the "colors of rhetoric," or between the composition of a painting and the design of a poet's story, his plot. Corre-sponding to the most noble forms of poetry, epic and tragedy, was the "grand style" in art, narrative painting such as Raphael's or Michelangelo's, and painters evidently thought of themselves

7

as storytellers, expecting their pictures to be "read" almost like texts. Conversely, poets evidently thought of themselves as bringing pictures to life. Think, for example, of *The Shepheardes Calender* in its original edition, each eclogue introduced by a woodcut presenting the characters and major symbols of the poem in visual form. In particular, think of the January eclogue, in which Colin's lament is set within a narrative frame in which Spenser sketches a verbal portrait of the shepherd against the pastoral landscape. In reading the poem we first examine Colin from a distance, noting his physical details and the details of the landscape, after which the picture comes alive and begins to sing. Milton uses the same technique throughout *Paradise Lost* and of course in *Lycidas,* where, after the eclogue proper, the poem resolves itself into a visual image of the shepherd against the background of the setting sun.[9]

The pictorial sensibility, the "visualizing imagination," that Shakespeare shares with most of his contemporaries is so basic to his way of thinking that naturally it affects every aspect of his dramaturgy. His verse, as we all know, is strewn with images, and I need hardly mention the frequency of formal "paintings" like Gertrude's description of Ophelia drowning or Enobarbus' portrait of Cleopatra on her barge. The pictorial sensibility also affects that aspect of his art that we perhaps think of as most dynamic, the presentation of character.

As Bernard Beckerman points out, Shakespeare is more interested in reaction, in response to events, than in motive and action.[10] This is one of the ways he shifts the emphasis from story to meaning, and it is also one reason his plays have considerable psychological interest. By modern standards, however, Shakespeare's techniques for the portrayal of response are notably static. The plays tend to show us discrete moments of intense emotion, "speaking pictures" of characters fearful, despairing, in love, jealous, raging, or rejoicing. Normally the reactive moment is dwelt upon for a full realization of the emotion: Romeo and Juliet falling in love, for example, or, for a more sophisticated illustration, Cleopatra bitchy and bored in Antony's absence.

Often these moments become little tableaux, for instance, Richard II upon his return from Ireland alternating between hope and despair; and often, too, as I have already suggested, they become emblematic, as in the graveyard scene in *Hamlet*.[11]

Generally speaking, a Shakespearean scene, when it is concerned with "character," will show us a figure in a given emotional posture, or assuming one, that is, switching from joy to grief, despair to hope, as change in fortune demands change in feeling. Such changes tend to be sudden, clearly marked, and complete, as when Juliet learns of Romeo's banishment. Changes in feeling—as abrupt as love at first sight—merge with more significant changes in "character," which also tend to be sudden and complete, such as Edmund's reformation or Leontes' jealousy. Most often, however, when Shakespeare wishes to show significant character development he allows the changes to occur offstage, giving us merely the "before and after" pictures. Usually the change is marked by the character's absence from the stage for a few scenes: the sleep-walking scene, for example, is the first time we have seen Lady Macbeth in six scenes. Very often, too, the change is marked by a journey—frequently with symbolic overtones—such as Romeo's journey to Mantua, Hamlet's sea voyage, or Lear's journey to Dover.

What I am suggesting is that the presentation of character in Shakespeare is perhaps less like a modern film in which the figures are in constant motion than an album of snapshot stills to be contemplated in sequence, each photo showing the subject in a different light, a different stage of development. Or, to translate the idea back into Elizabethan terms, Shakespeare normally presents character by showing us a series of speaking pictures. Through this method he forces us to juxtapose the different images of the character spatially—that is, in a single moment of perception—and to contemplate the meaning and mystery of the change, the difference between the iron-willed queen of the banquet scene in *Macbeth* and the distracted woman looking with horror at her hands.

In using the term "spatial" I am referring of course to Lessing's famous distinction in *Laocoon* between painting as an art of space and poetry as an art of time. Writing in the latter half of the eighteenth century, Lessing was attempting to demolish the whole idea of the sister arts, to prescribe the "natural" limits within which painting and poetry should confine themselves. Modern psychology suggests that Lessing's rigid distinction is misleading: we seem to perceive both arts spatially and temporally together.[12] But the scientific "truth" of the matter is perhaps less interesting than the fact that Lessing's ideas are indicative of that enormous shift in sensibility at the end of the eighteenth and start of the nineteenth centuries that we generally label the transition from neoclassic to romantic. If Renaissance writers tended to think of poetry spatially, in terms of painting, romantic writers tended to think of poetry more in terms of music, in terms of time.[13]

To speak of the spatial sensibility of the Renaissance and the temporal sensibility of the romantics and their heirs is a radical simplification, regardless of whatever truth the idea might have. Still, the notion can be helpful if handled gingerly. Certainly some of the more extreme nineteenth-century misreadings of Shakespeare can be better understood in this light. Would Mary Cowden Clarke ever have written *The Girlhood of Shakespeare's Heroines* if she had thought of Shakespeare's plays in terms of speaking pictures?

We are only just beginning to appreciate the degree to which Renaissance thought in general was spatially oriented—to understand, for example, that there is a connection between the addiction to the allegorical tableau and the spatial conceptualizations of Renaissance logic. More important for our present purposes, we are also beginning to appreciate the degree to which the Renaissance conceived of poetic form in spatial terms. The popularity of "shaped poetry" like Herbert's "Easter Wings" is symptomatic, and it may not be without significance in connection with our new understanding of Renaissance poetic form that in the last few decades this kind of verse has once again begun to appear, now called "concrete poetry."[14]

As Northrop Frye points out, when Spenser begins the last canto of Book II of *The Faerie Queene* with the words "Now gins this goodly frame of Temperance / Fairely to rise" he means that in addition to the narrative or temporal structure, a unified structure of meaning has been erected, a spatial structure like a painting or a building, which, now that the book is concluding, can be apprehended as a whole. "Such a passage," Frye says, "shows the principle of *ut pictura poesis* in action."[15] Indeed, a spatial sense of form seems to be fundamental to Spenser's art. As Frye elsewhere remarks, "Spenser is not, like Coleridge, a poet of fragments. Just as there is a touch of Pope himself in Pope's admiration for 'The spider's touch, how exquisitely fine!' so there is a touch of Spenser himself in Spenser's admiration for the honey bee 'Working her formal rooms in wexen frame.' He thinks inside regular frameworks—the twelve months, the nine muses, the seven deadly sins—and he goes on filling up his frame even when his scheme is mistaken from the beginning."[16]

The conception of *The Faerie Queene,* outlined in the letter to Raleigh, is just such a "wexen frame," or, to alter the metaphor, an elaborately organized cycle of paintings like Michelangelo's Sistine ceiling, with the twelve projected books devoted to the twelve private moral virtues ultimately to be balanced by a second series of books devoted to the public politic virtues. Moreover, as several recent critics have noted, the six completed books are themselves designed in terms of a symmetrical scheme that may be analyzed in a number of different ways. For example, Books I, II, and III (Holiness, Temperance, Chastity), presenting the virtues of the individual life, are balanced against Books IV, V, and VI (Friendship, Justice, Courtesy), presenting the virtues of life in society. Alternatively, the books fall into complementary pairs: I and II, which show so many parallels in structure, devoted to the inner life; III and IV, concerned with different aspects of love; and V and VI, again parallel in structure, opposing the social claims of law against those of courtesy. The first and final pairs thus form a frame around the central pair, III and IV, the two Ariostan books, which are very different from the others in technique and in which Queen Elizabeth's "descent" from Britomart and Artegall is celebrated.[17]

The structure of the *Epithalamion* has been much discussed of late, but whether or not we accept A. Kent Hieatt's numerological interpretation we are all familiar, I believe, with the basic symmetry of the poem, what William Nelson calls its "pyramidal structure." The poem moves from prayer to prayer, the opening invocation of the Muses, Nymphs, Hours, and Graces balancing the concluding prayers to Cynthia, Juno, Genius, Hebe, and the "high heavens." The rousing of the bride at the beginning is balanced by her bedding at the end. Her dressing in the morning balances her disrobing in the evening. And precisely in the center of the poem a speaking picture and central emblem for the *Epithalamion* as a whole, are the two stanzas which give us the image of the bride at the church altar, the priest blessing her and the angels hovering about her modestly downcast face while the organ plays and the choristers joyously sing. The overall structure is thus a patterned processional movement to and from the altar, with the second half of the poem designed to balance the first in series of motifs as well as in length.[18]

Spenser's approach to poetic structure is perhaps related to the practice of classical poets such as Vergil and Ovid, whose works are also symmetrically patterned.[19] It is obviously related, too, to medieval practice, such as Chaucer's never-completed scheme for *The Canterbury Tales*—two tales from each pilgrim on the way to Canterbury and another two on the way home. But it has very little to do with modern notions of "organic form." Spenser may be atypical in many ways—possibly in the elaborateness of some of his poetical schemes—but in his general approach to form he is more or less representative of his period.

Let me cite just one example. Marlowe's *Hero and Leander,* as Louis Martz has recently shown, is not a fragment, as it has usually been considered, but a complete poem, nicely designed in itself, and requiring no "continuation" by Chapman or anyone else to perfect it. Its structure becomes apparent, however, only in the edition of 1598 in which it was published by itself, without the division into "sestiads" and without the tetrameter "arguments" that Chapman added when he divided the poem. According to Martz, Marlowe's poem falls into a symmetrical triadic design. The opening section, running 384 lines, gives us the description of the lovers and their first encounter at the feast of Adonis. Next we have a mythological central panel of exactly 100 lines, the tale of Mercury, the country maid, and the Fates. And finally we have the consummation of the love, a section of 334 lines, roughly balancing the opening section in length. *Hero and Leander* thus has "the structure of a triptych, with the fable of the gods at the center and the story of the mortal lovers on either side." The mythological centerpiece is not a digression, but a demonstration of the power of love at work in the universe—a central emblem that provides the key to both structure and meaning.[20]

The structural pattern of the *Epithalamion* might perhaps be perceived by a mind attuned only to plot, for the two central stanzas in the church, the marriage itself, are in a sense the turning point of the "story." Needless to say, a purely narrative approach would miss much of the significance of the church stanzas' being in the center. But what would a critic with such an approach have to say about *Hero and Leander?* Probably he would perceive the poem as loose and episodic, and, if he were in a sour mood, he might chastise Marlowe for his digression about Mercury, possibly adding something about Elizabethan exuberance and love of copiousness. Certainly, he would never see the analogy between the two poems in structure, both depending upon symmetrical disposition of the parts around a significant centerpiece.

The structural pattern that the *Epithalamion* and *Hero and Leander* share is common in Renaissance poetry. We can find it, as I have already suggested, in the first six books of *The Faerie Queene,* where the two Ariostan books, III and IV, with their continuous narrative lines form a single great centerpiece concerned with love. And we can also find it in *Paradise Lost,* where, as has often been observed, Books VI and VII, dealing respectively with the war in heaven and the creation of the universe, form a great central diptych of destruction balanced against creation, or, rather, destruction transformed into creation, evil into good, on a cosmic scale.[21]

Remembering the tendency to assume a correspondence between the poet's design of his narrative and formal composition in painting, we should not be surprised to find that the same pattern of balanced design, often with an emblematic centerpiece, is also very common in early and high Renaissance painting, even when the painting is a single unified composition and not a series of panels like a triptych. We have only to think, for instance, of Botticelli's *Birth of Venus* or *Primavera*—both excellent examples, by the way, of paintings designed to be "read"—or Leonardo's *Last Supper*. Raphael's *School of Athens* will illustrate the point very well. In the center of the painting, framed by the last in the series of receding arches, stand the crucial figures of Plato and Aristotle, turned slightly toward each other as if in the midst of philosophical contention. Plato, who is on the viewer's left, points heavenward, indicating the transcendental nature of his philosophy, while Aristotle, on the right, extends his hand parallel to the earth, indicating the need to preserve the mean. The crowd of figures on Plato's side of the composition, dominated by the statue of Apollo, who inspires poetic frenzy, all represent writers and thinkers of a transcendental, Platonic inclination. The Platonists are balanced by the crowd of Aristotelians on the right—among whom Raphael has placed himself—dominated by the sterner statue of Minerva. The central figures, Plato and Aristotle, are thus not merely individuals but emblematic representatives of two complementary principles in human thought, and in them and their relation to each other is encapsulated the idea developed more largely in the painting as a whole. Roughly speaking, the purely structural function of the central figures in the painting as the emblem and pivot upon which the whole balanced composition turns is analogous to the structural function of the central stanzas of the *Epithalamion,* the central "panel" of *Hero and Leander,* or the central "diptych" of *Paradise Lost.*[22]

I am well aware of the dangers of facile parallel-hunting between poetry and painting, especially between Elizabethan poetry and Italian painting, and perhaps I should assure the reader even now that I have no intention of producing for his contemplation a "classical," "mannerist," or "baroque" Shakespeare. The various arts have individual traditions and concerns, and they do not necessarily develop along parallel lines. Moreover, England in the sixteenth century was a relatively provincial country in European terms—Italian painting was unfamiliar except to the very rich—and the theater in particular has always been a notoriously inward-looking, conservative art.

To find visual analogues to the common spatial patterns of Elizabethan poetry we do not, however, have to cross the Channel or even leave the immediate milieu of the poets and playwrights. The same patterns of balanced design and central emphasis were normal principles of organization for the elaborate allegorical *tableaux vivants* of the Lord Mayor's shows and royal progresses. They are also normal principles of organization for the more elaborate title pages, such as that for Ben Jonson's *Workes* (1616), which consists of a typically symmetrical screen façade with a woman representing "Tragoedia" standing between double columns on the left side and another representing "Comoedia" on the right, the two allegorical personages framing the title, which is surmounted by a theater and several other significant figures. Most interesting, the same principles can be seen in the disposition of the various elements of the public theater stage, particularly in the two columns supporting the heavens, and the two side doors, which frame the central "discovery space" used for the display of emblematic tableaux such as Ferdinand and Miranda playing chess in *The Tempest.* The evidence of the plays also implies that Elizabethan staging, the composition of the "stage picture," was markedly symmetrical, especially in the earlier period. In big scenes, when many actors were onstage, a central figure such as the king was generally selected as an emblem and focal point around which the other figures would be symmetrically arranged. Entrances and exits tended to bring significantly opposed characters on and off in balanced pairs from opposite doors, and sometimes dramatic logic was sacrificed to achieve this kind of symbolic symmetrical arrangement.[23]

What I am trying to suggest through these analogies between

structures in various art forms is not only the inseparability of form and meaning in Renaissance art generally but also that the same concern with proportion that characterizes Renaissance endeavor in the visual arts is reflected in the spatial organization of such nicely proportioned poems as the *Epithalamion* and *Hero and Leander*. In many ways the idea of "proportion" is the key to Renaissance aesthetics, and its importance in connection with Elizabethan poetry has not perhaps been generally understood.

We tend to think of "beauty" as subjective—"Beauty is in the eye of the beholder"—but the Renaissance concept, like the classical one from which it was partly derived, was objective and concrete: beauty consists in the harmonious relation of the parts to each other. Oversimplifying somewhat, we will not be entirely wrong if we think of beauty or "harmony" as equivalent to proportion, and proportion as often equivalent to symmetry. Or, as Alberti, in a famous passage puts it: "Beauty is a kind of harmony and concord of all the parts to form a whole which is constructed according to a fixed number, and a certain relation and order, as symmetry, the highest and most perfect law of nature, demands."[24] The reason a particular building or painting or statue, or, for that matter, a woman's face, is beautiful is because it observes this law of nature: it is harmoniously proportioned.

The Renaissance aesthetic had moral and metaphysical dimensions as well. The beautiful and the good could be identified because the most beautiful thing of all was God's cosmos, the various spheres moving in perfect "harmonic" relations. What Alberti means when he says that a beautiful building is constructed according to a "fixed number" as the "law of nature" demands is that such a building embodies the same ratios, the same proportions, as the universe itself: it is beautiful because, in a sense, it is a miniature of God's Creation.

Since beauty was supposed objective and subject to mathematical laws, it seemed possible to Renaissance thinkers to devise a sure and "scientific" way of designing pleasing buildings or paintings. One had only to discover the mathematical ratios of cosmic beauty and transfer them to art. Fortunately, these ratios were already understood, by the musicians, whose instrumental harmonies were pleasing because they, too, reflected the divine harmony of the cosmos. Transfer the concords of music—thirds, fifths, octaves, and such—to architecture or painting and one would produce beauty. Alternatively, one might go directly to those things in which nature shows herself most excellent, obtain measurements, and apply them to art. In particular one could go to man, certainly the most excellent thing in nature, and attempt to discover empirically, by actually measuring the human body as Alberti, Leonardo, and Dürer did, the secrets of proportion and consequently of beauty. The common "Vitruvian figure," of which Leonardo's drawing of a man with arms outstretched inscribed within a circle and a square is perhaps the most familiar example, is thus an emblem not only of human dignity but of the secret of all beauty and goodness.

The details of the Renaissance aesthetic, which was replaced by more subjective ideas of beauty at about the same time that the notion of the sister arts was replaced, are fascinating but need not delay us here. What we need to appreciate is merely that musicians, painters, sculptors, architects, and poets were all, in various ways, concerned with proportion. Remembering this, we can better understand why George Puttenham devotes the second of his three books in *The Arte of English Poesie* (1589) to "Proportion Poetical," and why he begins it by calling the mathematicians and theologians to witness that "all things stand by proportion" and that without proportion nothing can be good or beautiful.[25]

Proportion

Although the subject is not usually considered in the context of Renaissance aesthetics, most of us are familiar, I believe, with the nice proportions of certain of Shakespeare's plays. The symmetrical design of *A Midsummer Night's Dream,* for example, is particularly clear. We begin in the bright daylight world of Athens, the city of reason, exemplified by Theseus, the man who equates lunatics, lovers, and poets, taking none of them very seriously, since they are all more imaginative than reasonable. The daylight world is also exemplified by the Athenian law, which takes no account of Hermia's love for Lysander, very reasonably insisting that in a dynastic matter like marriage a girl should obey her father. In desperation the lovers flee to the forest, ruled by the fairies in whom only a lunatic or poet could believe, and the play's long middle section takes place in this enchanted nighttime world, illuminated by the fanciful gleam of the moon. Confusion follows confusion as one after the other of the lovers is anointed with the juice of the magic flower, and much of the hilarity of the central section derives from the young men's conviction that their sudden changes in affection are perfectly reasonable. At last a harmonious arrangement is achieved, with each of the girls matched to one of the men, just as the moon sets and the sun begins to rise, Theseus riding into the forest with his pack of well-tuned hounds. We return now to Athens for a reprise of the opening and a celebration of the multiple unions, and the quartet of lovers, having emerged from the moonlit forest, can finally sit with Theseus and his bride and laugh at the spectacle of love' However, lest we have doubts about the reality of the dream in the forest, Shakespeare brings on the fairies again for a brief coda at the end, for their existence, at least in this play, is as certain as the fact that the sun does not shine all the time or that Athens is not all the world.

The design of *A Midsummer Night's Dream* is thus triadic, like that of *Hero and Leander,* with the bright Athens panels framing the long moonlit centerpiece. As in *Hero and Leander,* the side panels are roughly equivalent in length, running approximately 250 and 350 lines respectively, the massive central panel running nearly 1,300 lines. The moonlit centerpiece, we should note, is a large speaking picture of what it means to be in love, a concrete representation of a rich metaphor with roots reaching deep into the Middle Ages: to be in love is to be wandering in confusion in an enchanted forest in the night.

This description of the play's design does not take into account the "rude mechanicals," Bottom, Peter Quince, and the other workmen. The design of *A Midsummer Night's Dream* is actually five-part rather than three-part, for placed between the two major Athens panels and the forest centerpiece are two minor panels, approximately 100 and 50 lines respectively, concerned with the workmen. The play's design can thus be more fully described as a double frame around the central panel:

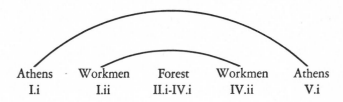

Athens	Workmen	Forest	Workmen	Athens
I.i	I.ii	II.i-IV.i	IV.ii	V.i

The Athenian workmen, would-be playwrights and actors, are notably short on imagination and long on plodding logic. They are, among other things, Shakespeare's burlesque of the purely rational sensibility represented by Theseus. Significantly, the workmen enter the forest to plan their play—the forest naturally suggests the world of the imagination as well as love—where they are wonderfully oblivious of their enchanted surroundings until Bottom is "translated" and they all run away in terror. As his name implies, Bottom is the most oblivious of them all: he converses with the fairies and makes love to their queen, never recognizing that anything much out of the ordinary is happening until the next morning when he has a vague intimation of having had a wonderful dream. Many have observed that Bottom and Titania represent the opposite extremes of the play, define those extremes in whatever way we wish. It is perhaps noteworthy, then, that it is in the very center of the forest sequence and the play as a whole that the extremes meet, that Titania falls in love with the ass and carries him off to her bower. This union can be interpreted in many different ways, depending upon how one defines the play's theme: the important thing for us is not so much what it means as where it comes—in the same position as the crucial church stanzas of the *Epithalamion* or the crucial figures of Plato and Aristotle in Raphael's painting.

The design of *A Midsummer Night's Dream* suggests a playwright with a strong sense of spatial form and quite remarkable powers of organization. The shapely proportions are approximate rather than exact, like those of *Hero and Leander,* indicating that Shakespeare did not normally count lines but that he did have a feeling for the general "mass" of a scene and knew when he was writing a long scene and when a short one. Very similar conclusions can be drawn from the design of *The Winter's Tale,* to choose another familiar example of a well-proportioned play.

The balanced structure of *The Winter's Tale* has often been examined, and, although there may be disagreement about how certain details are to be interpreted, the general organization is clear. The key to the design, as Ernest Schanzer among others has pointed out, is the Chorus, Time, who enters in the middle to divide the play into two parts separated by the gap of sixteen years. The two parts are roughly equal in length, the first running about 1,370 and the second about 1,550 lines. Time carries an hourglass, which exactly in the center of his speech he turns, marking the crossing of the wide gap. Both halves of the hourglass look alike, Schanzer notes, and the glass itself may be taken as an emblem of the play's shape.[26]

The two halves of *The Winter's Tale* correspond to each other in an elaborate system of parallels and contrasts. Each opens with a brief "prologue" in prose, the conversation between Camillo and Archidamus in the first half (I.i) and that between Camillo and Polixenes in the second (IV.ii). In each case the dialogue introduces a harmonious relationship soon to be disrupted, the friendship between the kings in the first half and the love between their children, Florizel and Perdita, in the second. Leontes' destructive jealousy in the first half is balanced by Polixenes' wrath in the second, and in both episodes the role played by Camillo is much the same: in the first case he warns Polixenes and helps him flee to Bohemia, and later he warns Florizel about his father's anger and helps the prince to flee with Perdita to Sicily.

The Winter's Tale has more than once been compared to a diptych. The first or winter panel is a miniature tragedy, except that

Leontes, unlike Othello, does not kill himself when he discovers his mistake but vows continual penance instead. The wintery half concludes with a symbolic recapitulation of the destructive forces in the foreground of this panel—the famous scene in which the storm sinks the ship and Antigonus is eaten by the bear. But the comic shepherds who enter midway through the scene to save the infant lying on the beach foreshadow the second movement, the spring panel, concerned with rebirth even as the first is concerned with death. "Now bless thyself!" the old shepherd says to his son, who has just witnessed the disasters at sea and on land, "thou mettest with things dying, I with things new-born" (III.iii.106–107). If the first panel is a tragedy, the second is a miniature comedy complete with angry *senex,* Polixenes—and here, naturally, youth and love, rather than death, are in the foreground. This movement, too, concludes emphatically, with the statue scene, approximately the same length as the seacoast scene, recapitulating the theme of rebirth. And just as the clowns on the seacoast qualify the tragic panel and foreshadow the comic half, so, at the end of the statue scene, Paulina looks back to the earlier tragedy, recalling her husband, Antigonus, and Shakespeare delicately reminds us that some deaths are real.

Acts and Scenes

We note that in neither *A Midsummer Night's Dream* nor *The Winter's Tale* does the conventional division into five acts have much to do with the play's actual structure. In both cases the basic designs are at least confused by chopping the plays into five acts, and in the case of *The Winter's Tale* in particular the craftsmanlike proportioning of the two panels is wholly obscured by placing the fourth act division just before the Chorus, the slightly longer second movement thus starting at IV.ii. In every way the act divisions discourage us from seeing the plays as they really are.

The much debated question of act division in Shakespeare has been a scholarly red herring, diverting attention from the real issues and seriously impeding our understanding of the plays' organization. The question whether Shakespeare knew and followed the Horatian five-act rule has probably seemed to many critics an arid subject, which they could afford to ignore. Possibly the issue has even discouraged some from embarking upon serious, inductive studies of structure. The subject *is* arid precisely because, as recent scholarship has demonstrated, act division plays no part at all in Shakespearean structure.[27]

Briefly, the situation is this. Throughout the Elizabethan period act division, as a supposedly classical practice, carried considerable prestige, at least in certain circles. Evidently the private theaters like Blackfriars interrupted their performances with musical "act" intervals, and the plays written for these theaters, such as Lyly's allegorical comedies, were generally divided, as were early humanist plays such as *Gorboduc*. Performances in the public theaters like The Globe were uninterrupted. Nevertheless, the academically minded "university wits," such as Marlowe, Kyd, and Greene, do seem to have divided their plays in deference to Horace. But since their divisions had no real structural significance, and, more important, since they bore no relation to conditions of performance in a theater without intervals, they were often lost in the transition from foul papers to prompt copy.

With the notable exception of Jonson, none of the popular dramatists who followed the university wits—that is, Shakespeare, Heywood, Dekker, and the host of minor writers—made any use of act division. Excepting Jonson, there is not a single surviving public theater play from 1591 to 1607 that was originally divided. After 1607, however, with the arrival of a new generation of playwrights, including Middleton, Beaumont, and Fletcher, most of whom, like Jonson, wrote for both the public and the private theaters, there appears to have been a gradual change of practice in the public theaters, until by 1616, the year of Shakespeare's death, act division had become universal and there were perhaps intervals in the public theaters as well. Old plays when revived were now adapted to the new fashion, and when printed these orginally undivided plays often had act divisions added to make them look more modern.

In Shakespeare's lifetime not one of his plays was published with division of any kind. The first divided edition is the 1622 quarto of *Othello,* and that is inconsistent, omitting any heading for Act III. The Folio of 1623 is also notoriously inconsistent: some plays are divided, sometimes in impossible ways; some are incompletely divided; and some are not divided at all. Our act divisions derive from those of the Folio, rationalized and completed by the eighteenth-century editors, most of whom simply assumed that every play must have five acts. Samuel Johnson knew better, and even though he preserved the divisions in his own edition, he warned his readers that they meant little, and that Shakespeare's actual unit of construction was what we would call the scene:

The settled mode of our theatre requires four intervals in the play, but few, if any, of our authour's compositions can be properly distributed in that manner. An act is so much of the drama as passes without intervention of time or change of place. A pause makes a new act. In every real, and therefore in every imitative action, the intervals may be more or fewer, the restriction of five acts being accidental or arbitrary. This Shakespeare knew, and this he practised; his plays were written, and at first printed in one unbroken continuity, and ought now to be exhibited with short pauses, interposed as often as the scene is changed, or any considerable amount of time allowed to pass. This method would at once quell a thousand absurdities.[28]

It is interesting to observe the "scene," defined as a cleared stage indicating change of place or lapse in time, emerge as the basic unit of construction in the popular dramatic tradition. In the early, more purely allegorical moralities in which nearly every character represents an abstract idea and normal conceptions of time and place are meaningless, the cleared stage has little or no structural importance. Sometimes, as in the very early *Hickscorner* (1513?), the stage is never empty. The cleared stage begins to become significant only in the latter half of the sixteenth century when "realistic" characters share the platform with the Vice and the old allegorical figures. In *King Darius* (1565), for example, there are four cleared stages, used to separate the pure "morality" scenes from the "historical" scenes. *All for Money* (1559–1577), which consists of a series of variations on the evils of money, uses the cleared stage in a similar fashion. Each section is in a different dramatic mode, so that we get pure allegory, débat, "realistic" exemplum, and biblical fable in turn, and with each shift in mode there is a cleared stage. Time and place begin to have value as the popular drama moves toward chronicle and romance in such plays as *Horestes* (1567), *Cambises* (c. 1558–1569), and *Clyomon and Clamydes* (1570–1583). In these plays the scenes become shorter and more numerous—there are thirteen scenes in *Horestes,* for example, and twenty-three in *Clyomon and Clamydes*—and the cleared stage is used in much the same way it is in Shakespeare.

It is plain both from certain passages in the texts and from the surviving manuscript "plots," those scene-by-scene outlines of the action which hung backstage for the company's use during a performance, that by the time of the great public theaters both playwrights and stage managers thought of plays as a series of scenes.[29] Even playwrights like Kyd and Marlowe, who nominally divided their plays into acts, actually constructed in scenes. However, just as most of our modern texts of Shakespeare persist in reprinting the confusing act divisions, so they are often seriously misleading in their division of the scenes.

The conventional scene divisions that we find in nearly every copy of Shakespeare we pick up are by and large the product of eighteenth- and nineteenth-century editors thinking in terms of an illusionistic picture-frame stage rather than the more flexible platform stage. Thus very frequently they mark divisions in the middle of continuous action, sometimes even when the stage is full. The fourth scene of *Romeo and Juliet,* to cite only a single familiar example, is still often printed as two scenes, I.iv, generally labeled "A street," and I.v, "A hall in Capulet's house." In the first segment of this scene Romeo and his friends enter masked and talk about dreams, Mercutio delivering the Queen Mab speech. The second segment is the ball, and between the two comes only the direction: "They march about the stage, and Servingmen come forth with napkins."

Nearly everything I have said on the subject of act and scene divisions in Shakespeare is well known, I trust, to most Shakespeareans. In fact I have done little more than outline the principles upon which the *Pelican Shakespeare,* the best edition in this respect that we yet have, is conceived. The reason I have bothered to repeat these scholarly commonplaces is to emphasize their importance, and to emphasize, too, the importance, especially in matters structural, of using a properly divided edition. Shakespeare's basic dramatic unit is the scene, and it is with the internal structure of individual scenes that discussion of design in the plays must begin. But just as it is impossible to perceive the structure of Marlowe's *Hero and Leander* in Chapman's edition, so it is almost impossible, for physical and psychological reasons, to perceive the structure of scenes in nearly all editions of Shakespeare, even when the editor assures us in a note that the act divisions mean little and that many of the traditional scene divisions should be ignored.

Although the scholarly foundation for an understanding of Shakespearean structure has lain ready for some time, we still approach the plays with a somewhat inappropriate mental "set." Symptomatic of this is the fact that we tend to think of the plays in terms of episodes rather than scenes: our terminology gives us away, our use of such phrases as the "recorder scene" in *Hamlet* or the "porter scene" in *Macbeth.* Neither of these episodes is, properly speaking, a scene.

Closely connected with our assumption that the plays are episodic is another assumption not subject to proof or disproof but certainly open to question. Granville-Barker's enormously influential *Prefaces* have trained us all, producers, actors, scholars, and general audience alike, to think of a Shakespeare play as a seamless, continuous spectacle to be performed, ideally, without pause or interval. Thus in our productions we often see the actors for one scene enter and begin speaking before the actors of the preceding scene have completed their exit. Sometimes a director even contrives to make the lines from two scenes overlap, presumably in order to bind the web as tightly as he can. The analogy of the movies has penetrated very deeply into our conceptions of how the plays ought to be performed, and indeed one is often explicitly told that the flow of action in an Elizabethan performance was curiously like that of modern films.

Granville-Barker's ideas about Shakespearean production represented a tremendous advance in simplicity and flexibility over the older traditions of "strong curtains" and operatic scenery, and the seamless-web approach may well be the most effective way to present Shakespeare to a modern audience. But this does not mean that it is historically accurate. On the contrary, the fairly evident connection between this approach and the anachronistic idea of "organic form" should lead us to suspect that it possibly is not. Johnson, we recall, recommended a short pause between the scenes, and in fact what little substantial evidence we possess suggests that it may well have been normal public theater practice to punctuate the scenes by allowing the stage to remain vacant for a few moments so that each scene could be absorbed as a whole before the actors began the next.[30]

The possibility that it was common practice to allow a pause between scenes is interesting in connection with the approach to Shakespearean structure that I shall outline in the following chapters. I shall suggest that we regard Shakespeare's scenes, the basic dramatic units of the plays, as individually designed compositions. Each scene is, in a sense, a single speaking picture: proceeding through a play is somewhat like proceeding past a cycle of narrative paintings, pausing to absorb each picture in turn before stepping back to discover the unifying principles of the cycle as a whole. The major pictures are themselves "multiple," that is, they are generally composed of a number of panels, distinguishable dramatic segments, related to each other in much the same way as the separate panels of a poem like *Hero and Leander*. Moreover, in many cases, major scenes show, on a smaller scale, the same evidence of careful craftsmanship, the same concern with proportion, as plays like *A Midsummer Night's Dream* or *The Winter's Tale*.

The Shakespearean Scene

The Integrity of the Scene

Our sense of structure in the plays is vague; our sense of structure in individual scenes is even vaguer. A Shakespearean scene, as we know, may be any length at all, from eight or nine lines to eight or nine hundred. To most of us the longer scenes perhaps seem little more than a series of episodes. Each episode is excellent in its own right, of course, and each somehow contributes to the play as a whole, but how closely are the episodes related to each other? Could not an episode placed at the end of one scene very often come just as well at the beginning of the next? Since we regard each play as fundamentally a seamless web, the breaks between the scenes probably seem of little importance, and we pay scant attention to where one scene ends and another begins.

Let us begin with a relatively simple scene from *Richard III,* which provides crude but correspondingly clear examples of how Shakespeare approaches his art. The fourth scene presents the death of Clarence, murdered in the Tower through Richard's Machiavellian intrigues. Strictly speaking, the scene is not required by the narrative: it might be omitted without in the least obscuring our understanding of who did what to whom and why. The play would be the poorer, of course; for one thing, it would lack a fine bloody spectacle, the murder itself. Yet blood and gore are not Shakespeare's fatal Cleopatra—recall that he does not bother to dramatize the murder of the little princes—and the nearly 300 lines that the scene runs constitute an altogether extravagant expense of verse for a mere murder.

The murder scene falls into two distinct segments. In the first Clarence relates to the jailor his prophetic dream of being at sea with Richard and being struck overboard and drowning. Beneath the sea Clarence sees an emblem of the vanity of earthly pride—heaps of gold, pearls, and jewels, scattered on the ocean floor—and, in the skulls bearing gems instead of eyes, an image of how men blind themselves to their own good. His moral sense revived by this *memento mori,* Clarence passes in his dream to hell, where the ghosts of those he has injured howl his wickedness in his ears, and he awakes trembling and frightened, a speaking picture of a man conscience-stricken. The second and longer segment of the scene is the actual murder, and much of the reason for the length here, almost 200 lines, is that at the moment of the act one of the murderers has qualms, a crisis of conscience. There follows a grotesque comic debate between the killers on the relative values of conscience and earthly reward—a counterpoint of course to Clarence's dream. Reward, naturally, wins, and the murderers proceed to dispatch Clarence. The scene's two segments, the dream and the murder, constitute complementary variations on a single theme—conscience.

The thematic, or, to be more precise, conceptual, integrity that this scene from *Richard III* reveals is normal for Shakespeare, and is, moreover, the kind of dramaturgy we might expect from a sensibility indebted to the morality plays. Shakespeare's scene divisions generally define units of meaning as well as units of narrative.

The sixth scene of *King Lear* is a more interesting example of this aspect of Shakespeare's art, and it is also a good example of how improper divisions can obscure important matters. This scene is still usually printed as three: II.ii, iii, and iv; II.ii gives us Kent's fight with Oswald, which results in his being put in the stocks; II.iii, Edgar's soliloquy in which he describes his plan to disguise himself as Poor Tom; and II.iv, Lear's discovery of Kent and his fight with his daughters, which results in his being shut out in the storm. The stage is never empty: Edgar's soliloquy takes place with Kent asleep in the stocks in full view of the audience.

When Shakespeare's scene is considered as a whole we can easily see that it is an integral unit. For one thing, the action takes place in a single, complete day, from the earliest morning of Oswald's

"Good dawning to thee, friend" (II.ii.1) to the late evening of
Gloucester's "Alack, the night comes on" (II.iv.295).[1] For another,
the principal narrative is continuous, the stocking of Kent leading
to Lear's quarrel with Regan and Goneril. If we are merely looking
for narrative coherence, however, Edgar's soliloquy must seem intrusive, an episode from the subplot placed here for little reason
except to give a sense of time passing before Lear discovers his
man in the stocks. In fact, the unity of the scene is thematic rather
than narrative. Each segment—the Kent section, the Edgar section,
and the Lear section—develops the same idea: each shows a good
man unjustly shut out in the cold, excluded from the castle. Turning
Lear out in the storm is of course a more drastic action than the
stocking of Kent, and we can observe that the segments increase in
emotional intensity as the scene proceeds.

Let us look for a moment at the Kent and Lear segments. They
are analogous in that each gives us a quarrel and an exclusion, and
the Kent segment is clearly meant to foreshadow the Lear episode,
to suggest that the king will not find comfort and love with Regan
any more than he has with Goneril. More interesting, the two
episodes are conceived in what almost seem different literary modes.
Kent and Oswald are simple characters so close to the morality
tradition that they might with little embarrassment bear labels instead of names, Good Service and Bad Service. The quarrel between
them actually has no motivation except their opposed natures, and
in this it recalls numberless morality contentions between a Virtue
and a Vice. Moreover, the stocking of Kent recalls a common motif
in the early drama, the fettering of Pity in *Hickscorner* or of Charity in *Youth*.[2] The morality-like Kent episode serves as a prologue
to the Lear episode, conceived in the normal tragic mode, and it
helps us to see that, despite the fact that the moral universe in this
segment is more complex, despite the fact that Lear is a "mixed"
character, not virtue embodied, he is nevertheless a man more sin-
ned against than sinning. In other words, the Kent segment helps
to determine our "angle of approach" to the Lear segment.

Between the scene's two major episodes is placed the "intrusive"
soliloquy, Edgar's description of how he will grime his face with

filth, tie his hair in knots, "And with presented nakedness outface / The winds and persecutions of the sky" (II.iii.11–12). The verbal portrait that Edgar paints of debased and brutalized humanity is an emblem crucially placed in the center of the scene, a prophetic picture of the consequences for humanity when the "holy cords" that bind parent to child, man to man, are rent asunder—the consequences when Good Service is put in the stocks and old men thrust out in the storm. The scene as a whole thus resolves itself into a triadic composition similar to *Hero and Leander* in which the two analogous side panels frame a central panel that comments on and explains them:

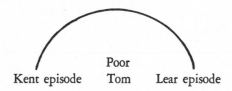

Kent episode   Poor Tom   Lear episode

One further point should be noted. The emblem in this composition is a verbal portrait, but there is also in the center of this scene a visual tableau. Outcast and hunted as a would-be murderer, Edgar believes that he has been abandoned by his family and friends. By convention he does not notice Kent, also an outcast, sleeping in the stocks. But the audience sees that Edgar is not alone. The point that is made here visually will be repeated later: Lear, too, believes that he is alone in the storm, deserted by everyone except a madman and a fool, but in fact Kent is at his side; and Gloucester, thrust out to smell his way to Dover, is tended at every step by Edgar.

Recognizing the principle of thematic, or conceptual, integrity within the scene is a preliminary step to understanding the design of scenes, and it is also a practical principle for the critic or teacher to keep in mind. One of the first questions to ask about a scene in which the episodes seem particularly diverse is whether it consists of variations on a single theme. Frequently, the answer will explain why an apparently detachable episode, like Edgar's soliloquy, is placed in one scene rather than another. Recognizing that scenes in

Shakespeare are generally devoted to particular themes can also, by itself, give us a firmer sense of a play's dramatic structure. A theme like "conscience" in *Richard III* does not merely emanate from the general "verbal texture"; it can be concretely located. The conscience theme is introduced in I.iv, after which, except for a few passing references, it is more or less dropped until the end of the play when the ghosts appear to Richard in his sleep at Bosworth Field and he awakes, like Clarence, conscience-stricken. Richard soon recovers, however, echoing the second murderer when he proclaims that "Conscience is but a word that cowards use" (V.iii.310). The strategy of raising and then dropping the theme makes for effective moral drama, for no idea so emphatically introduced can be forgotten, and the play's long silence on the subject becomes itself significant.

Design in the Scene

Most of us are familiar with certain obviously patterned scenes in Shakespeare. The distinctive thing about these scenes is how inorganic they are in structure: design is imposed upon the dramatic material from without, according to a preconceived plan, rather than being allowed to develop from within. The result is a rather brittle, plainly artificial, dramatic structure of a kind not much to modern taste.

Conspicuously patterned scenes are especially common in the early plays. Perhaps the best known example is the seventh scene of *Love's Labor's Lost* (IV.iii) in which the academicians discover that they are all in love, all forsworn. The scene begins with Berowne ruminating upon the sonnet he has sent Rosaline. When the king enters, Berowne stands aside and listens as he reads his own declaration of love, the sonnet he has written to the French princess. Next the king stands aside and overhears Longaville read his sonnet to Maria, after which Longaville steps aside and overhears Dumaine read his sonnet to Kate. Here the action pivots and reverses itself, Longaville advancing to denounce Dumaine, the king denouncing Longaville, Berowne denouncing the king, and finally

Costard and Jaquenetta appearing with Berowne's own incriminating sonnet. Approximately midway through the scene Berowne sums up the situation:

> Sweet lords, sweet lovers, O, let us embrace!
> As true we are as flesh and blood can be;
> The sea will ebb and flow, heaven show his face:
> Young blood doth not obey an old decree.
> We cannot cross the cause why we were born;
> Therefore, of all hands must we be forsworn.
> (IV.iii.209–214)

And now, in the second half of the scene, which roughly corresponds to the first in length, the gentlemen decide to renounce their academy and woo the ladies. The scene as a whole is thus as structured as a dance:

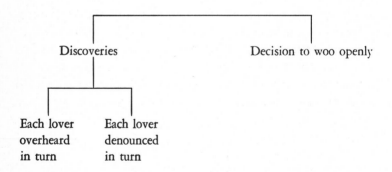

Another conspicuously patterned scene is the Battle of Towton sequence in *3 Henry VI*, which contains the famous episode in which Henry soliloquizes in the middle of the battle and overhears the complaints of a son who has killed his father and a father who has killed his son. This sequence is usually printed as four scenes, II.iii-vi, but like most battles in Shakespeare it is designed as a whole and the patterned composition of the unfortunate father and unfortunate son is part of a larger scheme.

The scene opens with alarums and excursions, after which the chief Yorkists—Warwick, Edward, Clarence, and Richard—in turn rush onstage defeated and fleeing. Richard, however, rallies his comrades and the fight begins anew. Next, while the battle rages offstage, we have Henry's soliloquy and the father-son episode. Finally the prince and queen report that the Lancastrians have lost and Henry must fly, after which the Yorkists return, proclaim their victory, and triumph over their fallen enemies. The sequence as a whole thus consists of two paired battle segments which frame the emblematic centerpiece:

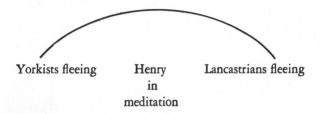

Yorkists fleeing   Henry   Lancastrians fleeing
                             in
                        meditation

The centerpiece is the key to the significance of the scene and indeed to the conception behind the entire play. It begins with the king meditating upon the battle and remarking how, like the sea —a frequent image in Shakespeare for fortune and disorder—it sways first in one direction, then another. Next Henry dreams of the shepherd's peaceful life. He pictures himself carving a sundial—here a symbol of natural order—and using it to regulate every aspect of his life:

> So many hours must I tend my flock,
> So many hours must I take my rest,
> So many hours must I contemplate,
> So many hours must I sport myself;
> So many days my ewes have been with young,
> So many weeks ere the poor fools will ean,
> So many months ere I shall shear the fleece.
> So minutes, hours, days, weeks, months, and years,
> Passed over to the end they were created,
> Would bring white hairs unto a quiet grave.
> Ah, what a life were this! how sweet, how lovely!
>   (II.v.31–41)

33

The regulated, progressive motion of the life he envisions contrasts with the swaying tides of the battle, fortune merely sweeping first in one direction and then another without purpose or goal. This meaningless existence, the centerpiece suggests, is not the end for which months and years were created. Nor were sons meant to kill fathers or fathers sons: this dual emblem defines the horror at the heart of civil war.

Formal patterning of the sort that is most conspicuous in early plays like *Henry VI* or *Love's Labor's Lost* is not a technique that Shakespeare discards as he matures, any more than he discards the "artificiality" of blank verse. Nearly all major scenes in the mature plays are patterned, some very elaborately. Among other things, patterning is a technique Shakespeare uses to give weight and emphasis to important scenes, and since these scenes tend to be long, generally 250 to 400 lines, the overall scheme helps to shape the various episodes within each scene into a unified composition. Yet, even as Shakespeare's verse grows more supple and fluid while retaining its essential formal qualities, so his scenic technique becomes increasingly more "natural," and, not understanding the formal principles of Shakespearean design, we may be tempted to suppose there are no formal principles at all.

As we shall see in later chapters, the most interesting scenes from the point of view of design normally fall at three places in the play, the beginning, the middle, and the end. The importance of the opening scene is a commonplace of Shakespearean criticism: especially in a "narrative" or "extensive" or "nonclassical" form of drama, that is, one that begins well before the crisis, the opening scene must bear the entire burden of establishing the play's tone and unifying themes, as well as introducing most if not all of the major characters. Usually the opening scenes tend to be "big" scenes—often the setting is the court—requiring the services of nearly the entire company, including supernumeraries. Sometimes, however, the opening scene, technically speaking, is not the first scene in the play. Most of Shakespeare's plays begin with some form of prologue in which the major characters do not appear, although usually they are discussed. Sometimes, this prologue is designed as part of the opening scene, as for example in the opening of *Lear,* where the brief conversation between Gloucester, Kent, and Edmund leads directly into the court episode in which Lear divides the kingdom. Often, however, the prologue is a scene in its own right, as in *Julius Caesar,* where the processional opening scene is preceded by the brief scene in which Flavius and Marullus lecture the commoners about Pompey and Caesar. The longest and most elaborate prologue in Shakespeare is the battlements scene of *Hamlet,* which precedes the opening scene proper. The importance of the finales is obvious, although in the history plays these are frequently abrupt compared to the comedies or tragedies. Perhaps less commonly realized is the fact that in the middle of Shakespeare's plays we can usually expect to find a third major scene— the mousetrap in *Hamlet* or the temptation scene in *Othello*— which is normally the turning point in the action and is generally emphasized by elaborate formal patterning.

I expect that many have sensed, if perhaps vaguely, that the opening scene of *Lear* is somehow formally patterned, yet the usual approaches to Shakespearean structure do not provide the terms for understanding its design. In order to analyze this scene —like every other in Shakespeare—we must think of it both temporally, as a developing sequence of events, and spatially, as a structure that can be perceived as a whole.

The scene begins quietly and privately with the brief prologue. The first few lines introduce the main plot and the situation in the kingdom:

> *Kent.* I thought the King had more affected the Duke of Albany than Cornwall.
> *Gloucester.* It did always seem so to us; but now, in the division of the kingdom, it appears not which of the dukes he values most, for equalities are so weighed that curiosity in neither can make choice of either's moiety. (1–6)

The fact of the kingdom's division is dropped casually—it is a given, a situation not discussed because it is taken for granted— but precisely because it is so understated, both here and in the body of the scene, it reverberates uneasily: division of a social unit, a kingdom or a family, is not a thing to be taken so casually. What the conversation focuses on is Lear himself, specifically on his judgment, his choices between men. The king had always seemed to prefer Albany to Cornwall—his instinct was sound, as we will later learn—but now it appears as if he makes no distinction between them. The issue is value, the relative worth of men. The conversation next focuses on Edmund, as Gloucester presents his son to Kent, joking about his bastardy. Edmund is pointed at and discussed, treated as an object for contemplation: the idea of judgment has already been raised and, implicitly, we are being asked to judge Edmund, to consider just how "proper" the issue of Gloucester's "fault" really is. Once again the casual tone is at odds with the implications of the situation: Shakespeare is trying to suggest the easy ignorance with which one stumbles into destruction.

The prologue, which runs 33 lines, is balanced by an epilogue roughly equivalent in length. After the long, ceremonial court episode, Cordelia and France remain behind for a word with Goneril and Regan. Cordelia indignantly denounces her sisters, predicting that time will unfold their real natures to the world. In the design of the scene, this conversation corresponds to the earlier Gloucester-Kent conversation about Edmund: again we are being asked to consider and judge the characters before us, in this case the villains of the main plot. Through the design, Shakespeare is subtly suggesting the analogy between Edmund and the hypocritical sisters. Next, Cordelia and France exit, and the sisters, left alone, discuss their father and the untrustworthy judgment he has just revealed: "You see how full of changes his age is. The observation we have made of it hath not been little. He always loved our sister most, and with what poor judgment he hath now cast her off appears too grossly" (288–291). This conversation, which like the prologue is in prose, corresponds to Gloucester and Kent's opening exchange concerning the king's preferences between Albany and Cornwall. The scene thus opens and closes with our attention directed to Lear's judgment, but, whereas the prologue is casual, the epilogue is tense, focusing now on the fact that choices have consequences: "We must do something, and i'th'heat" (306).

In general outline, then, Shakespeare's design consists of two brief "private" segments which frame the large "public" segment that is the heart of the scene:

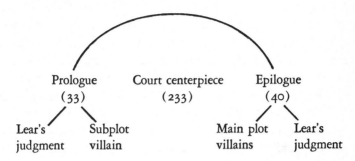

The private segments, with three and four characters respectively, are boldly distinguished from the body of the scene in which the stage is full, the royal presence accompanied by a train of attendants, and the ceremonial entrances and exits marked by formal flourishes. The dramatic contrast between the frame and centerpiece obviously enhances the scene's effectiveness on the stage. By dramatically establishing the distinction between public and private, the scene's structure also helps draw our attention to one of the play's central concerns. In particular, it helps direct our response to Lear, a man so confused about this fundamental distinction that he demands a public statement of his daughters' affections in return for acknowledging them as his children. Indeed, one of the crucial discoveries, perhaps *the* crucial discovery, that Lear will make in the course of the play is that the distinction between public role and private self exists, that he is not only a king but a man and no more ague-proof than the meanest wretch.

The long court centerpiece is also symmetrically patterned, composed of three segments once again arranged according to the frame principle. What we have here in fact is a triad within a triad—a very common pattern in Shakespeare's scenes. The centerpiece opens with the formal love-tests of the daughters. The king's inability to perceive the distinction between public profession and genuine love creates a dilemma for Cordelia. There is no way she can properly obey Lear's command and convince him that she loves him best, for, all the words of love having been debased by her sisters in their fulsome speeches, the only act that remains to her is eloquent silence, but this Lear rejects as "nothing." The episode mounts to a climax as Lear angrily withdraws the public symbols of his affection—once again he makes no distinction between the sign and the thing itself—banishing Cordelia from his heart.

The opening episode of the centerpiece, concerned with the relative worth of Cordelia, presents us with contrasted examples of interested and disinterested love, the ambitious sisters speaking to gain their portions and the loving Cordelia who refuses to speak. The closing episode, which brings on Burgundy and France to judge dowerless Cordelia's worth, is similar, except that here the contrasted figures are the judges rather than the judged. France, in perceiving Cordelia's value even though she is presented to him with none of the usual public signs of worth, illustrates the way Lear ought to have acted earlier. These two analogous panels, each a love test, are equivalent in length, running 87 and 79 lines respectively, and frame the central episode in which Kent dares to come between the dragon and his wrath in order to rescue the king from error:

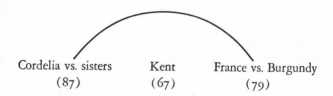

Cordelia vs. sisters   Kent   France vs. Burgundy
(87)   (67)   (79)

In approximately the middle, both of the central panel and of the scene as a whole, Kent bluntly states the concept that unifies the scene and forms the starting point in the play's homiletic structure: "See better, Lear" (158).

The myth of Shakespeare as an inspired natural, warbling his native woodnotes wild, has been exploded many times, yet it continues to haunt us, especially in discussions of structure. Great art cannot exist without inspiration, but in matters of structure Shakespeare is more the calculating architect than the inspired singer carried away by the beauty of his song. The shapeliness of the *Lear* opening, the symmetry and careful proportioning, is the mark of a master craftsman. If Shakespeare scarcely blotted a line, he must have planned scenes very thoroughly in advance.

The formal patterning of the *Lear* scene reflects Shakespeare's didacticism as much as his desire to tell a good story—the two purposes, to instruct and delight, are indistinguishable. Sometimes, however, we will find a disparity between the narrative line and the dramatic design, which allows us to measure the distance between Shakespeare's purely narrative concern and his concern with meaning. The scene in which Macbeth murders Duncan is a good example. Readers may have sensed the patterning of the *Lear* opening, but it is unlikely that many have sensed the patterning of this scene, in part because it is generally divided into three, II.i, ii, and iii. Properly, the long series of events including Macbeth's midnight encounter with Banquo, the dagger soliloquy, the murder and the following conference with Lady Macbeth, the porter episode, Macduff's arrival, and the rousing of the sleeping guests should be considered a single scene. Twice in the scene the stage is momentarily cleared, when Macbeth exits to kill the king and just before the porter's entrance, but in neither case is there a change of time or place and the action is plainly continuous.

The scene's narrative structure is simple: the action leads up to and then away from the murder, Shakespeare showing us first Macbeth steeling himself for the crime and then the reactions—Macbeth's horror, Lady Macbeth's icy control, and finally the shock of the Scottish nobles as they learn the king is dead. The crux of the narrative, the turning point, is of course the murder itself. This, however, takes place offstage, and it also comes notably early in the scene, about one-fifth through. The crux in the dramatic design, the central panel, is not the murder but the porter's soliloquy, which Coleridge so disliked because it seemed to him intrusive, a violation of the scene's otherwise solemn tone. Before the porter episode comes a series of private, surreptitious, conspiratorial comings and goings, including the murder, which runs 137 lines. After the central panel comes another long segment, balancing the first, the public displays of horror as the nobles assemble. The sense of time in the scene is well marked and it is important. The first long panel takes place sometime after midnight, that is, in darkest night, an appropriate time for murder. By the time of Macduff's entrance, however, it is dawn, and with the first light come recognitions of many kinds.

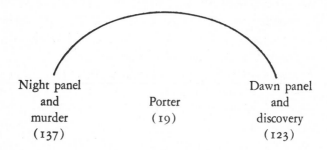

Night panel
and
murder
(137)

Porter
(19)

Dawn panel
and
discovery
(123)

The function of the porter is chiefly to suggest the significance of the events of the night. Like Edgar's soliloquy in the sixth scene of *Lear,* to which it is analogous structurally, the "intrusive" porter's speech provides a speaking picture that serves as a central emblem for the scene. What the disparity between the narrative and dramatic structures reveals is the degree to which Shakespeare's attention is on meaning, how in imposing a formal pattern on the action he is also imposing an interpretation.

Let us examine the action somewhat more closely. The scene begins with Banquo's entrance, preceded by Fleance carrying a torch. The torch and the opening conversation about the moon's setting establish the time and mood. Good actors will also be able to suggest the symbolic significance of this torchlight entrance: it is that time of night when men stumble and lose their way. Thinking of the weird sisters, Banquo has been driven from his bed by horrid thoughts, evidently of murder:

A heavy summons lies like lead upon me,
And yet I would not sleep. Merciful powers,
Restrain in me the cursed thoughts that nature
Gives way to in repose.   (II.i.6–9)

Banquo's chief role at the start of this scene is as foil to Macbeth:
Shakespeare is reminding us that although it is difficult to resist
temptation, it is not impossible. Immediately after the "heavy
summons" speech Macbeth enters, also preceded by a torchbearer.
The visual parallel between the two pairs onstage reinforces the
deeper analogy: Macbeth, too, has been thinking of the sisters,
though he quickly denies it when Banquo mentions them. The
men nervously part, wishing each other "good repose," a thing
unattainable for either; but whereas Banquo will remain awake
to restrain his thoughts, Macbeth is about to act.

The scene's first long movement from Banquo's entrance to the
porter's is a single mounting nightmare. Shakespeare has organized the segment so that Macbeth and Lady Macbeth seem to be
constantly coming and going, giving an effect of fretful, fearful
activity. The panel is filled with images of howling wolves, ghosts,
and shrieking owls, and with mysterious visions and voices, the
dagger that Macbeth cannot grasp—among other things it suggests
the elusiveness of his goal, which is not just to murder Duncan
but to be truly king—and the voice that cries, "Sleep no more!"
The climax of this movement is the insistent knocking that terri-
fies Macbeth and drives him and Lady Macbeth off the stage. There
is nothing supernatural about this knocking: it is only Macduff
come to wake the king. Nevertheless, given the circumstances,
the knocking seems portentous, like fate itself at the door, and,
in a sense, it is fate, for Macduff is the man who will ultimately
destroy Macbeth. The mysterious and the commonplace interpene-
trate in this scene, so that we can hardly tell which is stranger,
Macbeth's dagger of the mind or Macduff's knocking. As in *The
Winter's Tale* where Shakespeare sets in motion the opposed ideas
of art and nature, showing art continually resolving itself into nature, nature into art, so in *Macbeth* he sets in motion the opposition
between the familiar and the strange until the two become indistin-

guishable. That which seems mysterious, like the prospect of Birnam Wood coming to Dunsinane, turns out to be simple and natural; whereas that which seems simple, like the murder of a king, turns out to be not so simple.

The entrance of the porter drops us abruptly from the world of high tragedy to that of low comedy, from the extraordinary and noble to the base and commonplace. And yet the porter is not merely a clown: as Glynne Wickham among others has pointed out, he is the descendant of the figure of the porter of Hell Castle familiar in the "Harrowing of Hell" plays of the old mystery cycles.[3] Macbeth has damned himself, and the picture that Shakespeare puts at the center of this scene is a grotesque image of hell:

Knock, knock, knock. Who's there, i'th'name of Belzebub? Here's a farmer that hanged himself on th'expectation of plenty. Come in time! Have napkins enow about you; here you'll sweat for't. (*Knock.*) Knock, knock. Who's there, in th'other devil's name? Faith here's an equivocator, that could swear in both the scales against either scale; who committed treason enough for God's sake, yet could not equivocate to heaven. O come in, equivocator. (*Knock.*) Knock, knock, knock. Who's there? Faith here's an English tailor come hither for stealing out of a French hose. Come in, tailor. Here you may roast your goose. (*Knock.*) Knock, knock. Never at quiet! What are you? —But this place is too cold for hell. I'll devil-porter it no further. I had thought to have let in some of all professions that go the primrose way to th' everlasting bonfire.   (II.iii.3–18)

The foolish farmer, the treacherous equivocator, and the thieving tailor all suggest aspects of Macbeth's crime. In the comic perspective of the porter's speech, Macbeth is no longer the grand, mysterious tragic figure of a moment before but only one more in the long line of ignorant or self-deceiving souls marching to the everlasting bonfire.

One way in which this long scene is unified is by repetition of motifs in the night and dawn panels, a technique that emphasizes the scene's balanced design. Once in each panel the stage bell rings—in the night panel it summons Macbeth to his act; in the dawn panel it rouses the house. In each case the ringing is immediately followed by the entrance of Lady Macbeth, who holds center stage while her husband is busy in the royal chamber, murdering Duncan in the night panel and the grooms in the dawn panel. More important, the scene is unified by the dominant image of broken sleep, which suggests the psychological and social, as opposed to the specifically religious, implications of the murder. Macbeth has divorced himself forever from nature's renewal:

> Methought I heard a voice cry 'Sleep no more!
> Macbeth does murder sleep'—the innocent sleep,
> Sleep that knits up the ravelled sleave of care,
> The death of each day's life, sore labor's bath,
> Balm of hurt minds, great nature's second course,
> Chief nourisher in life's feast.   (II.ii.34–9)

In the night panel the sleep theme is primarily verbal, although the spectacle of Banquo and Macbeth restlessly wandering about the castle by torchlight starts the scene with a strong visual image. The dawn panel in which the various sleepers stumble onstage wearing nightgowns provides the literal fulfillment of the verbal imagery of the first segment: Macbeth's act has disrupted not only his repose but that of all Scotland. The use of the sleep image to unify this scene is analogous to the use of the conscience motif in the *Richard III* murder scene, and, as in *Richard III*, the emphatic introduction of the motif here prepares us for a later scene— Lady Macbeth's sleepwalking.

Frame Scenes and Diptych Scenes

The same patterns occur again and again in Shakespeare's work. The *Macbeth* murder scene, the opening scene of *Lear*, the Battle of Towton, and the scene in which Kent is put in the stocks and the king turned out in the storm—each of these is designed on the frame principle, the same general pattern that we observed earlier in *A Midsummer Night's Dream*, in which the two Athens panels frame the great forest centerpiece. Much can be learned about Shakespeare's art by noting the kinds of material he places in the emphatic central positions in these designs. In the *Lear* opening, Kent's direct statement, "See better, Lear," is at the heart of the scene. In the Kent in the stocks scene, the Battle of Towton, and the murder scene it is also a conceptual rather than a narrative element that is emphasized, but in these cases instead of direct statement Shakespeare gives us images, Edgar's portrait of brutalized humanity, Henry's pastoral vision balanced against the horrific reality of the father and the son, the porter's evocation of hell. In structural function these emblematic centerpieces are analogous to the church stanzas at the center of Spenser's *Epithalamion* or the figures of Plato and Aristotle in the center of *The School of Athens*.

The framing pattern of *A Midsummer Night's Dream* is one of the two basic designs Shakespeare most often employs in scene composition. The other is the diptych pattern of *The Winter's Tale* with its winter and spring halves. The simpler diptych pattern is especially common in the earlier plays, where scenes frequently fall into two major segments balanced against each other, as in the forswearing scene of *Love's Labor's Lost* or the conscience scene of *Richard III,* the speaking picture of Clarence conscience-stricken paired and contrasted with the image of the hired killers who decide not to meddle with conscience. In structure the diptych scenes are analogous to, say, Michelangelo's *Fall* in the Sistine chapel, where the figures of Adam and Eve appear twice in the single composition: on the left side of the picture they take the apple from the serpent, on the right they are driven from the garden. "Look here upon this picture, and on this" is the thought silently present.[4]

The opening of *Romeo and Juliet* is a good example of a diptych scene, the vain feud between the Capulets and Montagues balanced against Romeo's vain love for Rosaline. The scene begins with Samson and Gregory, two Capulet servants, picking a very silly quarrel with two Montague servants. Foolish though it is, the quarrel develops into a serious disturbance of the peace as more and more characters enter and are drawn into the fight, until at last the prince appears and in a formal speech restores order, reproving Capulet and Montague and requiring that they each appear at "old Freetown, our common judgment place" for a final disposition of the matter. After the prince's speech the stage is cleared except for Montague, Lady Montague, and Benvolio. The second segment begins with a brief recapitulation of the quarrel, Montague inquiring who began the fray. But almost before Benvolio can finish his description of the events Lady Montague inquires about her son: "O, where is Romeo? Saw you him today? / Right glad I am he was not at this fray" (I.i.114–115). The mention of Romeo's name brings forth a burst of word-music, the shift in theme from hate to love being signalled by the marked shift in tone which Granville-Barker likens to "a change from wood-wind, brass and tympani to an andante on the strings."[5]

> Madam, an hour before the worshipped sun
> Peered forth the golden window of the East,
> A troubled mind drave me to walk abroad;
> Where, underneath the grove of sycamore
> That westward rooteth from this city side,
> So early walking did I see your son.   (116–121)

The verbal overture to Romeo's entrance continues for several dozen lines, as Benvolio and Montague draw a vivid picture of the young man's melancholy, after which the lover appears and proclaims his passion for Rosaline in affected paradoxes. The prince's reproof of Capulet and Montague has its counterpart in Benvolio's reproof of Romeo for persisting in a futile passion, and the scene ends with Benvolio vowing to cure his friend's obsession.

The scene as a whole thus falls into a "hate" panel and a "love" panel of roughly equivalent lengths, 101 and 135 lines respectively, dramatically distinguished by the group exit of some seventeen or so characters and attendants after the prince's speech. The scene is designed to suggest that the feud and Romeo's passion are equally silly and, perhaps, equally dangerous as well, both forms of "heavy lightness, serious vanity." Possibly, too, we have here an early attempt to produce an effect similar to that of the opening scene of *Lear,* in which the scene's design, dramatically distinguishing between behavior in private and in public, helps to draw our attention to the king's confusion on this matter. The *Romeo and Juliet* scene distinguishes clearly between hate and love, but the characters do not. As many critics have noted, the bawdy clowning of Sampson and Gregory significantly opens the scene with a conflation of brawling and loving.

> *Sampson.* I will take the wall of any man or maid of Montague's.
> *Gregory.* That shows thee a weak slave; for the weakest goes to the wall.
> *Sampson.* 'Tis true; and therefore women being the weaker vessels are ever thrust to the wall. Therefore I will push Montague's men from the wall and thrust his maids to the wall.
> *Gregory.* The quarrel is between our masters, and us their men.
> *Sampson.* 'Tis all one. I will show myself a tyrant. When I have fought with the men, I will be cruel with the maids—I will cut off their heads.
> *Gregory.* The heads of the maids?
> *Sampson.* Ay, the heads of the maids, or their maidenheads. Take it in what sense thou wilt. (I.i.10–25)

The servants' clowning perhaps has its counterpart in the second panel in Romeo's Ovidian description of his "attack" on Rosaline:

> She'll not be hit
> With Cupid's arrow. She has Dian's wit,
> And, in strong proof of chastity well armed,
> From Love's weak childish bow she lives unharmed.
> She will not stay the siege of loving terms,
> Nor bide th'encounter of assailing eyes. (206–211)

To Romeo, as to the servants, the whole world of emotion still seems, as he says, a chaos of brawling love and loving hate. Like the creating word dividing darkness from light, Juliet's sun-like appearance at her window will divide brawling from loving, the daylight of the soul from the night. The discovery of genuine love will make the distinction between hate and love clear.

The great final scene of *Othello* is another diptych scene, analogous in structure, if in no other way, to the *Romeo and Juliet* opening or the overall pattern of *The Winter's Tale*. Like the "hate" and "love" panels of the *Romeo and Juliet* scene, the two panels of the *Othello* finale are distinguished by the number of characters onstage. The first half of the *Romeo and Juliet* scene is crowded, the second half more intimate. This is a common pattern in Shakespeare's opening scenes, just as the reverse, for obvious reasons, is common in the finales. For example, the opening scene of *Hamlet,* that is, the scene after the battlements prologue, gives us first a crowded court episode and then the intimate conversation in which Horatio tells Hamlet about the ghost. The finale reverses the pattern, giving us first an intimate conversation with Horatio together with the Osric episode, after which we have a crowded court segment, the duel with Laertes.

In the first panel of the *Othello* finale the Moor smothers Desdemona and then defends his act to Emilia. Emilia's cries for assistance—"Help! help! Ho! help! / The Moor has killed my mistress! Murder! murder" (V.ii.167–168)—abruptly fill the stage in approximately the middle of the scene, as Montano, Gratiano, Iago, and "others" come running. The intimate first panel is thus balanced against the more public second panel, in which Othello discovers that Iago has deceived him and commits suicide.

The scene begins with Othello's tormented soliloquy: "It is the cause, it is the cause, my soul. / Let me not name it to you, you chaste stars! / It is the cause" (1–3). The precise meaning of these lines is problematic, but most commentators agree that Othello is thinking of himself as the scourge of heaven, justly executing judgment upon his wife for her unspeakable crime. Indeed, a moment later he kisses Desdemona and presents himself abstractly as Justice personified: "O balmy breath, that dost almost persuade / Justice to break her sword" (16–17). The crisis of the first panel, the smothering, comes exactly in the center, at line 84. Desdemona does not die immediately, however, but toward the end of the panel momentarily recovers, reasserts her innocence, and then takes the responsibility for her death upon herself:

Desdemona. A guiltless death I die.
Emilia. O, who hath done this deed?
Desdemona. Nobody—I myself. Farewell.
　　Commend me to my kind lord. O, farewell! (123–126)

The contours of the second panel are similar to those of the first, the dramatic "shape" once again defined by a crisis, the murder of Emilia, which forms the turning point of the segment. The panel begins with Emilia fiercely confronting Iago, demanding justice for her slain mistress: "Disprove this villain, if thou be'st a man. / He says thou told'st him that his wife was false" (173–174). Refusing to hold her tongue, Emilia, after some 60 lines of violent argument, reveals how the crucial handkerchief came to Cassio's hands, and this husband-wife conflict, like that of the first panel, ends in death as Iago suddenly stabs his wife. The moment of Emilia's death is also the moment of Othello's recognition, as crying "Precious villain!" he attempts to kill Iago.

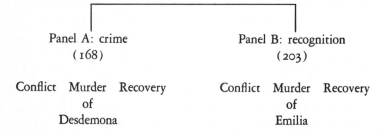

Panel A: crime   Panel B: recognition
(168)   (203)

Conflict Murder Recovery   Conflict Murder Recovery
of   of
Desdemona   Emilia

Othello now is on the rack indeed, torn in an agony of self-incrimination: "Whip me, ye devils, / From the possession of this heavenly sight! / Blow me about in winds! roast me in sulphur! / Wash me in steep-down gulfs of liquid fire!" (278–281). Before the scene ends, however, Othello momentarily recovers his composure, reasserting his dignity by reminding the Venetians of his service to the state, and publicly assuming responsibility for his crime:

> Speak of me as I am. Nothing extenuate,
> Nor set down aught in malice. Then must you speak
> Of one that loved not wisely, but too well;
> Of one not easily jealous, but, being wrought,
> Perplexed in the extreme; of one whose hand,
> Like the base Judean, threw a pearl away
> Richer than all his tribe. (342–348)

In the first panel the Moor painfully executes judgment upon his wife; in the second, with equal devotion to justice, he executes judgment upon himself, committing suicide. The scene as a whole is designed to emphasize his consistency, and, at the end, it comes full circle as Othello himself calls attention to the analogy between his two acts: "I kissed thee ere I killed thee. No way but this, / Killing myself, to die upon a kiss" (358–359).

The Tavern Scene

The patterning of scenes obviously serves a variety of purposes besides simply organizing each scene into a unified composition. As anyone who has written verse knows, it is often easier to compose in a formal pattern, ottava rima or heroic couplets, than in free verse: among other things, the requirements of the pattern help to generate poetic material. Robert Frost compared free verse to playing tennis without a net, by which he probably meant that without rules there is no sport, no sense of difficulty overcome. In point of fact, it is easier to play tennis with a net than without, for the net provides something to aim at, a guide in measuring one's strokes. Except in the extremely improbable event that a Shakespearean manuscript is one day discovered, we will never know very much about his actual working methods, yet it seems to me at least possible that Shakespeare found formal patterning of scenes an aid to composition. Clearly he found it helpful in establishing meaningful analogies between characters and situations, between the stocking of Kent, for instance, and the shutting out of Lear. Recognizing the design of a scene can thus be a practical aid to the critic in deciding how to interpret a particular episode. The design of the *Othello* finale, for example, suggests that T. S. Eliot's provocative remark about Othello's last great speech—that Othello is cheering himself up, endeavoring to escape reality—is perhaps, as Eliot feared, subjective in the extreme.[6] Not that we can ever escape subjectivity in criticism. Let me emphasize that I am by no means proposing a "scientific" approach to Shakespeare: many different interpretations can shelter under one analysis of design, and long scenes can often be analyzed in more than one way. Yet there are degrees of subjectivity, and the more we know about Shakespeare's art, his technique, the more firmly we can establish a common ground for interpretation of the plays.

Analysis of many scenes, including some of the greatest, reveals that long scenes are often built with combinations of the two basic designs, the framing pattern and the diptych. Small, individually designed units are combined like atoms in the formation of a molecule. The scene itself may be enormously complex, but the elements of which it is composed are quite simple. The second tavern scene, II.iv, in *1 Henry IV,* one of the greatest comic scenes in world literature and surely the greatest Shakespeare wrote, is an excellent example. Coming close to the center of the play, the tavern scene forms the turning point in the action. Before it, the play's major concern is whether—or, more precisely, when—Hal will forsake Falstaff and the tavern world to assume his place in history; after it, the play's concern is directed toward the Battle of Shrewsbury and Hal's ultimate triumph over Percy, his "robbery" of Hotspur's honors. Like that of every masterpiece, the genius of this scene, the spirit that gives it life, is finally mysterious. Much as we try, we can never quite put our finger on the pulse that makes the fat knight so vital, makes him Falstaff. To analyze the structure of a scene like this one is not to discover what makes it great, but merely to observe how the several elements in the scene relate to each other and what sense of purpose the design of the whole reveals.

The scene begins with Hal describing to Poins how he has been carousing with the tavern tapsters and in a mere quarter of an hour has learned their whole tongue, so that now he can "drink with any tinker in his own language" (18). Language is the major theme of Hal's speech, in particular the verbal poverty of simple people whose entire vocabulary consists of a few elementary phrases. But there is a secondary theme as well, and one that will soon become important—time. To "drive away the time" (26) till Falstaff comes, Hal conceives the practical joke on Francis, himself and Poins simultaneously demanding the tapster's attention in order to mock his predictable one-note response: "Anon,

anon, sir." The theme of verbal poverty continues through the Francis episode, but, as the joke progresses, it becomes increasingly subordinate to the emerging theme of time. All Hal's questions, we note, are concerned with some aspect of time: the length of Francis' indenture, his age, the day when he will have his reward for the sugar, and, finally and explicitly, "What's o'clock, Francis?"—to which the boy comically replies, "Anon, anon, sir" (92–93). Interpreted psychologically, Hal's behavior here casts him in an unpleasant light as a snide bully. But the principal thrust of the episode is emblematic rather than psychological: in Francis Shakespeare expects us to recognize a comic image for the prince himself, called simultaneously in two directions, the tavern and the court. The manner in which the episode gravitates toward the temporal theme reflects the increasing pressure that time is bringing to bear on Hal as the Percy conspiracy gathers to a head. The prince's responsibilities are calling and his reply so far has been the same as Francis': "Anon, anon, sir"—not yet, but soon.

The Francis episode is followed by a return to the situation and theme with which the scene opened; again Hal is alone with Poins, discoursing about verbal poverty, marveling that Francis should have "fewer words than a parrot" (94–95). This remark leads to a speech that may at first seem a non sequitur, for Hal suddenly thinks of Hotspur and announces that he is not yet of Percy's mind: "he that kills me some six or seven dozen of Scots at a breakfast, washes his hands, and says to his wife, 'Fie upon this quiet life! I want work'" (98–100). But if we have understood the emblematic significance of the game with Francis it should not seem strange that Hal's thoughts fly to Percy. Nor is the comment actually a non sequitur: Shakespeare juxtaposes the remarks about Francis and Hotspur so that we will understand that Hal's objection is Percy's lack of words, his intellectual poverty. The prince imagines Lady Percy requesting the daily body count and Percy answering, "Some fourteen"—to which he adds, after an hour of silence, "a trifle, a trifle" (103–104). Hal's vision of Percy is of course grossly unfair, as the audience who have just seen Hotspur and Kate in action are aware, but this need not concern us here. What is important is to notice that immediately after rejecting Percy—and, implicitly, the world of action and responsibility—as stupid, Hal calls for Falstaff, the man of wit, words, and inaction, who represents to him the opposite pole of humanity from wordless Francis and Percy. For now Hal's answer to his responsibilities is still a very firm "not yet."

Falstaff's entrance at line 107 marks the end of the first part of the tavern scene, which is designed, as we can now see, on the framing principle, the two Hal-Poins segments framing an emblematic central panel, the Francis episode. The language theme is dominant in the side panels, the time theme in the central panel.

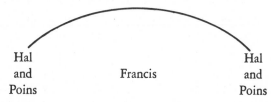

Hal	Francis	Hal
and		and
Poins		Poins

If Shakespeare had wished, this section might have stood by itself as a separate scene, but in fact it is only the prologue to the major part of the scene, the initial statement of themes. The prologue is not detachable, however, but an integral part of the scene's design. Part of its function becomes clearer when we realize that this unit as a whole is a single panel in a larger diptych structure, Hal and Poins' baiting of wordless Francis balanced against their baiting of wordy Falstaff as they prompt him to ever more ridiculous assertions about his courage at Gadshill.

Initially it appears that Falstaff, like Francis, is a man of one note, or rather two—"A plague of all cowards" and "Give me a cup of sack."

> *Poins.* Welcome, Jack. Where hast thou been?
> *Falstaff.* A plague of all cowards, I say, and a vengeance too! Marry and amen! Give me a cup of sack, boy. Ere I lead this life long, I'll sew netherstocks, and mend them and foot them too. A plague of all cowards! Give me a cup of sack, rogue. Is there no virtue extant? (107–112)

But Falstaff's repetitions emerge from a context of most un-Franciscan expansiveness and verbal play. As the episode progresses he creates out of nothing, out of mere words, an entire army of men in buckram suits: the exact contrary, we should note, to the Hotspur of Hal's imagination, who through verbal poverty reduces a genuine army to "a trifle." Our response as we watch Falstaff at his vocation can perhaps best be described in vitalist terms: after the narrow, mechanical, constrained world of Francis and Hotspur in the first episode, we find ourselves in the presence of something organic and alive, and the effect is of release into sudden freedom. There is high comic drama here. Hal and Poins are seeking to expose Falstaff, to trap him and tie him down to the world of facts, but from every snare they throw he escapes with the creation of more and still more absurd men in buckram suits. The climactic moment comes when they run him to a stand and advance with a "plain tale" to put him down:

We two saw you four set on four, and bound them and were masters of their wealth. Mark now how a plain tale shall put you down. Then did we two set on you four and, with a word, outfaced you from your prize, and have it; yea, and can show it you here in the house. And, Falstaff, you carried your guts away as nimbly, with as quick dexterity, and roared for mercy, and still run and roared, as ever I heard bullcalf. What a slave art thou to hack thy sword as thou hast done, and then say it was in fight! What trick, what device, what starting hole canst thou now find out to hide thee from this open and apparent shame? (240–251)

Triumphantly, Falstaff responds with the fable of the lion that will not touch the true prince. With a word he outfaces Hal and Poins from their prize.

The contrasted Francis and Falstaff panels complete the first major movement. We are just midway in the scene when the hostess tumbles onstage to announce that there is a messenger from court to speak with the prince. In Falstaff's orgy of words the pressure of time and responsibility has been forgotten, and now it reasserts itself. Falstaff makes a joke about the impropriety of old men being out of bed at midnight, and Hal, instead of re-

ceiving the message in person, significantly dispatches Falstaff to
send the man packing. Hal may still be hiding from the open and
apparent facts of his life, but the messenger's arrival is no less po-
tentous than the meteors and exhalations of Bardolph's nose,
which are discussed while Falstaff is offstage. Falstaff returns with
the news that the rebels are gathering and the prince must go to
court in the morning. Hal replies with quips about instinct and
the price of maidenheads; nevertheless, his situation has changed
radically and he knows it: a definite limit has been set upon the
duration of his holiday.

The principal action of the second half of the scene is the brief
play in which Falstaff and Hal take the role of king by turns. We
can observe how careful Shakespeare is to weave the structure of
his scene as tightly as he can, to leave no loose ends but connect
everything to everything else, by noting that twice in the first half
he has provided hints that some such episode as this is to come. It
is perhaps worth noting, too, as evidence for Shakespeare's feeling
for lucid design, that one hint is given in each of the two panels
of the first half and that in each case it is the final element in the
episode. At the end of the Francis episode Hal wants to stage a
burlesque in which he plays Hotspur to Falstaff's Dame Mortimer; and at the end of the Falstaff episode the triumphant knight
suggests a "play extempore" (265), to which Hal agrees, offering Falstaff's cowardice as a suitable subject. The effect of these
hints is to lead us toward accepting the second half of the scene
as the fulfillment of the first, and also perhaps to keep in our
minds the idea of playing and acting as the tavern world's alternative to action and work.

Hal and Falstaff's play continues the language theme. The
comedy of the episode lies in Falstaff's absurdity in the grand role
of king, an incongruity dramatically suggested by the mock heroic
expansion of a joint stool into a throne, a dagger into a scepter,
and a cushion into a crown. These physical incongruities com-
plement Falstaff's mock heroic expansion of language into a
travesty of regal grandeur, his hilarious speech in King Cambises'
vein, a parody of Lyly's euphuistic style:

Harry, I do not only marvel where thou spendest thy time, but also how thou art accompanied. For though the camomile, the more it is trodden on, the faster it grows, yet youth, the more it is wasted, the sooner it wears. That thou art my son I have partly thy mother's word, partly my own opinion, but chiefly a villainous trick of thine eye and a foolish hanging of thy nether lip that doth warrant me. If then thou be son to me, here lies the point; why, being son to me, art thou so pointed at? (380–389)

"Dost thou speak like a king?" Hal finally objects: "Do thou stand for me, and I'll play my father" (412–413). Falstaff as king is an incongruous fantasy, a pleasant sport; Hal playing his father is another matter entirely. The prince assumes the role in the spirit of the game, but at some point—it is up to the actors to decide when and how this occurs—both Hal and Falstaff realize that it is no longer quite fantasy that they are enacting, and the game acquires an uncomfortable edge.

Hal's deposition of Falstaff is of course a symbolic act. All through the scene this "tun of man," as Hal calls him, this "swoll'n parcel of dropsies," this "huge bombard of sack," has been almost visibly growing, expanding before our eyes, as he first swells himself into a hero battling buckram hoards, and then into the king himself, grandly chastising his wayward son. But all this growth is without substance; like the great belly itself it is all fat and no muscle, the mere froth of sack and gaseous fermentation of airy nothing, of words. Falstaff responds to Hal's half-serious denunciation of him as an abominable misleader of youth with a torrent of words in his own defense, begging him to banish Peto, Bardolph, Poins, but not sweet, kind, true, valiant, and old Jack Falstaff: "Banish plump Jack, and banish all the world!" (455–456). Hal's reply is the pricking of an Orgoglio. After all the swelling verbiage of this wordy scene, the prince suddenly speaks with the laconic simplicity of a Hotspur: "I do, I will" (457). After the vast edifice of fantasy that Falstaff has constructed, the hard facts of who Hal is and what he must do become again open and apparent. I do not underestimate the pathos of this moment, but its principal effect, I believe, is parallel to that of the climax of the first half of the scene when the cornered Falstaff bursts the constraints of fact, triumphantly escaping Hal and Poins' trap with his fantastic claim that like a lion he knew the true prince all along. The effect then was of release, and so it is here, except that this time the elements are reversed, and it is not from the world of fact but from the fogs of fantasy that we are freed.

Hal's four-syllable speech is followed, according to a generally accepted conjectural emendation, by the sound of knocking. Off-stage knocking in Shakespeare normally carries associations of fate, of something inevitable demanding to be admitted, as, for example, in the *Macbeth* murder scene, where the knocker is Macduff. The knocker here is the sheriff, the representative of law and responsibility, who is seeking Falstaff in connection with the Gadshill robbery. Falstaff loudly objects to the termination of his sport—"Play out the play. I have much to say in the behalf of that Falstaff" (460–461)—but plainly the fun has been spoiled. Plainly, too, the respite that Hal grants Falstaff by permitting him to hide while he outfaces the law is only temporary and the debt that riot owes to order will ultimately have to be paid—before dinnertime the next day, to be precise.

The sheriff is the second messenger from the outside world to intrude upon the tavern in this scene, and we can see now that the second half of the scene is designed on the frame principle, the two messengers framing the centerpiece in which the picture of Falstaff as king is balanced against the picture of Hal as king.

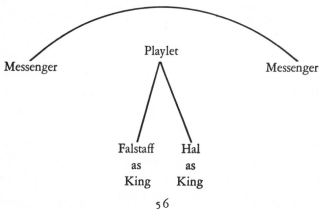

Once again the hostess rushes in frantically with words almost identical to those she used before to announce the messenger from court: "O Jesu, my lord, my lord!" (462). Once again the pressure of time and responsibility reasserts itself after having been forgotten in a game of words. This time, however, instead of dispatching an agent to send the man packing, Hal receives the sheriff onstage. Moreover, on this occasion he shows that he knows the time and takes it seriously. "Good night, my noble lord," says the sheriff in parting. The prince corrects him: "I think it is good morrow, is it not?" "Indeed, my lord, I think it be two o'clock" (498–500).

The sheriff's departure concludes the scene proper, but, as he often does at the end of a long scene, Shakespeare provides a brief coda to sum up the position to which the preceding action has brought us. Drawing aside the curtain behind which Falstaff is hidden, Hal discovers him asleep and snoring, characteristically unconcerned about the reckoning he must eventually face. In his pocket Peto finds another reckoning that Falstaff has ignored, his tavern bill, which is read aloud so that Hal may remark, "O monstrous! but one halfpennyworth of bread to this intolerable deal of sack!" (514–515)—a comment which suggests in a phrase much of what our latest perspective on Falstaff has shown. "I'll to the court in the morning" (517), says Hal, reminding us of his own reckoning and of the moral distance now between himself and the snoring Falstaff. And, with a significant repetition of good-morrows between Hal and Peto, a final insistence on the lateness of the hour, the segment and the scene ends.

The tavern scene, concerned throughout with the opposed pressures on Hal, is no less unified in theme than the conscience scene of *Richard III*, even if its subject cannot be so easily summed up in a single word. As the scene progresses, the two basic motifs, time and language, introduced in the Francis episode, become more and more suggestive as they gather associations with a chain of opposed motifs, including stupidity-wit, responsibility-irresponsibility, work-play, action-acting, fact-fantasy, and finally expansiveness and freedom versus limitation and reckoning. Furthermore, as the scene progresses, the smaller "atomic" units, like the

Francis episode, are steadily absorbed into larger and larger structures, until at the end the scene as a whole resolves itself into a single large design based on the diptych or balanced segments principle. The first half, running 268 lines, provides an increasingly positive perspective on Falstaff, contrasting his witty intelligence with Francis and Hotspur's dullness, and climaxing in Falstaff's triumphant escape from Hal and Poins' trap. The second half, running 255 lines, provides an increasingly negative perspective on Falstaff, reaching an equivalent climax in Hal's assertion that he will banish plump Jack.

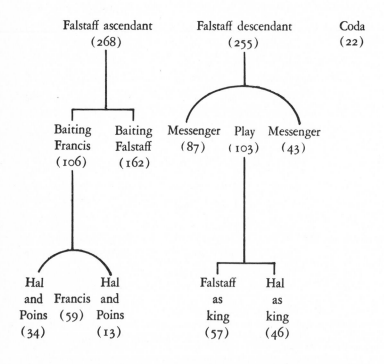

As in the *Othello* finale, we come full circle at the end. We begin with Hal and Poins alone onstage and, after a great deal of activity, of coming and going in which many actors are involved, we end with Hal and Peto. It is often noted that whereas scenes in plays written for a proscenium stage generally end at a moment of great dramatic tension, Shakespeare's tend to continue past the climax, ending with a gradual lowering of the dramatic temperature. A Shakespearean scene normally begins and ends in relative quiet, inscribing a parabola of excitement, or perhaps two parabolas as in the Kent in the stocks scene, where the action rises and falls twice, the dramatic structure reflecting the analogy between the Kent and Lear segments. This parabolic pattern is of course related to the exigencies of the curtainless stage, where the action cannot be halted abruptly because the actors have to talk their way off the deep platform. But Shakespeare does not construct scenes in parabolas merely because he has to: as always he turns technical problems to positive account, in this case using the coda to carry us back to the beginning of the scene in order to emphasize the contrast between Hal's position then and his position now. This procedure of returning full circle at the close contributes greatly to our sense of the scene as a complete dramatic unit.

Rhetoric and Symmetry

The "full circle" technique is a miniature version of the phenomenon familiar in so many of the plays as a whole, where the end echoes or in some way harks back to the beginning. At the end of *Lear,* for example, the royal family—Lear, Cordelia, Goneril, and Regan—is reassembled onstage for the first time since the opening scene. In the final tableau, however, all are dead. At the end of *Macbeth* the tyrant again dons the armor in which he first appeared. This time, however, he is the enemy rather than the protector of Scotland. Alternatively, we can view the full circle technique as an expanded version of the rhetorical figure termed *epanalepsis,* the repetition at the end of a clause or sentence of the word with which it begins. Like all the figures of repetition, epanalepsis is very common in Shakespeare: "Cassius from bondage will deliver Cassius" (*Julius Caesar,* I.iii.90), or "Purpose so barr'd, it follows, / Nothing is done to purpose" (*Coriolanus,* III.i.148–149).[7]

Training in rhetoric encouraged Elizabethan writers to think in such formal patterns, and nothing is easier than to find analogies to Shakespeare's principles of scenic structure on the rhetorical level. One of his favorite figures, for example, is *antimetabole,* which turns a sentence or phrase around to form a structure analogous to what I have called the diptych or balanced segments: "Plainly as heaven sees earth and earth sees heaven" (*The Winter's Tale,* I.ii.314) or "The fool doth think he is wise, but the wise man knows himself to be a fool" (*As You Like It,* V.i.30–31). And epanalepsis gives us many examples of framing, such as Gaunt's deathbed complaint to Richard: "Ill in myself to see, and in thee seeing ill" (*Richard II,* II.i.94). Rhetorical terminology was extremely well developed in the Renaissance, and no doubt it could provide us with a precise language for describing many aspects of Shakespeare's dramaturgy.

The rhetoricians were naturally concerned, too, with larger units than the phrase or sentence, and very often entire speeches or groups of speeches reveal the same principles of design as the scenes. The player king in *Hamlet,* for example, formally addressing his wife on the subject of constancy, calls attention to the way his own speech comes full circle at the end. He begins his speech by stating that purpose is the slave of memory, an idea he develops and illustrates for some 20 lines, after which he restates his thesis in different terms:

> But, orderly to end where I begun,
> Our wills and fates do so contrary run
> That our devices still are overthrown;
> Our thoughts are ours, their ends none of our own.
> So think thou wilt no second husband wed,
> But die thy thoughts when thy first lord is dead.
> (III.ii.202–207)

The player king's speech thus becomes a kind of rhetorical emblem, an example of memory and constancy of purpose.

Naturally it is in the early plays that we find the most conspicuous examples of rhetorical patterning within whole dramatic segments. *Titus Andronicus*, for example, opens with the equivalent on the rhetorical level of the scenic diptych. Saturninus and Bassianus enter from opposite doors, and each calls upon his followers to support his claim to the throne:

A
(8 lines)

Saturninus. Noble patricians, patrons of my right,
  Defend the justice of my cause with arms.
  And, countrymen, my loving followers,
  Plead my successive title with your swords.
  I am his first-born son that was the last
  That ware the imperial diadem of Rome.
  Tnen let my father's honors live in me,
  Nor wrong mine age with this indignity.

B
(9 lines)

Bassianus. Romans, friends, followers, favorers of my right,
  If ever Bassianus, Caesar's son,
  Were gracious in the eyes of royal Rome,
  Keep then this passage to the Capitol;
  And suffer not dishonor to approach
  The imperial seat, to virtue consecrate,
  To justice, continence, and nobility;
  But let desert in pure election shine;
  And, Romans, fight for freedom in your choice. (I.i.1–17)

The parallel speeches contrast the princes and their claims—Saturninus insisting upon simple primogeniture, Bassianus insisting upon the principle of election and invoking moral worth. Saturninus, as we know, will turn out to be a tyrant: already in the paired speaking pictures of the opening, the difference between the brothers is implicit.

The third speech of *Titus Andronicus* reveals framing. Marcus Andronicus enters aloft with the crown and announces that the tribunes and senators have committed their power of election to Titus:

A
(7 lines)

Princes that strive by factions and by friends
Ambitiously for rule and empery,
Know that the people of Rome, for whom we stand
A special party, have by common voice
In election for the Roman empery
Chosen Andronicus surnamed Pius
For many good and great deserts to Rome.

B
(14 lines)

A nobler man, a braver warrior,
Lives not this day within the city walls.
He by the Senate is accited home
From weary wars against the barbarous Goths,
That with his sons, a terror to our foes,
Hath yoked a nation strong, trained up in arms.
Ten years are spent since first he undertook
This cause of Rome, and chastised with arms
Our enemies' pride. Five times he hath returned
Bleeding to Rome, bearing his valiant sons
In coffins from the field.
And now at last, laden with honor's spoils,
Returns the good Andronicus to Rome,
Renowned Titus, flourishing in arms.

A'
(7 lines)

Let us entreat by honor of his name
Whom worthily you would have now succeed,
And in the Capitol and Senate's right,
Whom you pretend to honor and adore,
That you withdraw you and abate your strength,
Dismiss your followers, and, as suitors should,
Plead your deserts in peace and humbleness.   (18–45)

Two sentences, each seven lines long, open and close the speech,
framing the 14-line centerpiece. In the first sentence Titus' authority is proclaimed; in the last Marcus calls for the princes' ac-

quiescence; in the emphatically placed central section he describes Titus' accomplishments.

The following speeches, which return our attention to the princes, reveal another symmetrical scheme.

A

Saturninus. How fair the tribune speaks to calm my thoughts.

B
(9 lines)

Bassianus. Marcus Andronicus, so I do affy
In thy uprightness and integrity,
And so I love and honor thee and thine,
Thy noble brother Titus and his sons,
And her to whom my thoughts are humbled all,
Gracious Lavinia, Rome's rich ornament,
That I will here dismiss my loving friends:
And to my fortune's and the people's favor
Commit my cause in balance to be weighed.

B'
(7 lines)

Saturninus. Friends that have been thus forward in my right,
I thank you all and here dismiss you all,
And to the love and favor of my country
Commit myself, my person, and the cause.
Rome, be as just and gracious unto me
As I am confident and kind to thee.
Open the gates and let me in.

A'

Bassianus. Tribunes, and me, a poor competitor. (46–63)

Looking closely at the two central speeches in this segment (B, B'), we find that in the first Bassianus affirms his faith in the Andronici and then dismisses his men; in the second Saturninus performs analogous actions in reverse order, first dismissing his men and then affirming his faith in Rome. The segment as a whole is thus organized on the principle of *chiasmus,* or mirror symmetry, the last two speeches reflecting a reversed image of the first two. The scheme implicitly asks us to compare Saturninus' proud, distrustful one-line speech (A) with Bassianus' humble request (A'). It also emphasizes the difference between Bassianus' warm affection for the Andronici and Saturninus' colder, more abstract, profession of faith in "Rome."

These three segments constitute the play's prologue, which, as we can now see, is designed on the framing pattern, the two opening speeches balancing the closing speeches and together framing Marcus' verbal portrait of Titus' greatness:

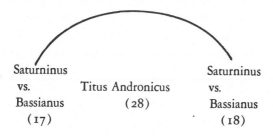

Saturninus   Saturninus
vs.   Titus Andronicus   vs.
Bassianus   (28)   Bassianus
(17)   (18)

This scheme obviously "places" Titus as the pivotal, central figure. At the same time, the precision of the scheme makes even minute details become significant. It is perhaps no accident that in the opening segment it is the aggressive Saturninus who speaks first, pressing his claim, whereas in the final segment the more honorable Bassianus is first to yield and dismiss his men. Bassianus commits his cause "in balance to be weighed," and it is perhaps no accident, too, that in each side panel he has a line or two more than his brother. Possibly Shakespeare is subtly tipping the metrical scales in his favor just as he has subtly tipped the moral scales.

If we think of Shakespeare's principles of scenic design as an extension of Elizabethan rhetorical practices we can see that there are interesting analogies to be drawn between, say, the balanced design of the *Othello* finale and Lyly's patterned prose with its balanced correspondences within the sentence. Almost any passage chosen at random from *Euphues* will do for an example:

Ah, fond wench, dost thou think Euphues will deem thee constant to him, when thou hast been unconstant to his friend? Weenest thou that he will have no mistrust of thy faithfulness, when he hath had trial of thy fickleness? Will he have no doubt of thine honour, when thou thyself callest thine honesty in question? Yes, yes, Lucilla, well doth he know that the glass once crazed will with the least clap be cracked, that the cloth which staineth with milk will soon lose his colour with vinegar, that the eagle's wing will waste the feather as well of the phoenix as of the pheasant, that she that hath been faithless to one will never be faithful to any.[9]

Constant-unconstant, faithfulness-fickleness, honor-honesty—Lyly's characteristic use of rhythm, alliteration, and assonance to articulate the symmetrical antitheses of his sentences is not entirely unlike Shakespeare's use of "alliterating" episodes—the murder of Desdemona, the murder of Emilia—to articulate the symmetrical design of his scenes.

Lyly and Sidney, especially the latter, were regarded as models of applied rhetoric, but obviously the rhetoricians cannot be held totally responsible for engendering euphuism or the analogous Arcadian style. The elaborately patterned prose of the 1580's and 1590's is perhaps best understood as another manifestation of the Renaissance concern for proportion, or, to put it somewhat differently, of the Elizabethan love of elaborate symmetry in all the arts, a taste most obvious in architecture and the other arts of design. But this aspect of Elizabethan taste is itself perhaps best understood as a manifestation of something else, a deeper and older current, the general tendency to organize all aspects of the world according to abstract symmetrical patterns—the four elements of physics (air, earth, fire, and water); the four humors of physiology (melancholy, phlegm, blood, and choler); the three ages of history (nature, law, and grace). Confronted with a formal or intellectual problem of any kind, the natural tendency of the Elizabethan sensibility seems to be to construct a symmetrical pattern.

Although so far as I know the subject has never been systematically discussed, we are all familiar with certain aspects of Shakespeare's symmetrical imagination. Especially in the early plays, he enjoys symmetrical replication of characters, the doubles of *The Comedy of Errors,* for example, in which he reveals his fundamentally Elizabethan sensibility by doubling the Dromios as well as the Menaechmi, or, for further examples, the double brace of lovers in *A Midsummer Night's Dream* and the quadruple in *Love's Labor's Lost.* And, of course, throughout his career, he continues a frequent practitioner of the double plot, balancing, for instance, the story of Gloucester and his sons against that of Lear and his daughters.

These are outward aspects of the plays. More interesting perhaps are the inward aspects of his thought. Norman Rabkin has suggested that what is most characteristic of Shakespeare's thought is not an ideology but a mode of vision—Rabkin calls it "complementarity"—which projects plays in terms of polar opposites such as reason and passion, reason and faith, reason and imagination, hedonism and responsibility, the world and the transcendent, justice and mercy. "Always the dramatic structure sets up the opposed elements as equally valid, equally desirable, and equally destructive, so that the choice that the play forces the reader to make becomes impossible."[10] I am not entirely convinced that the choice is always impossible to make. The claims of justice in *The Merchant of Venice* are great, but the claims of mercy are greater. But Rabkin's point that the Shakespearean imagination projects itself in pairs is surely right, and often we can find very concrete support for his thesis in the design of individual scenes.

In every aspect of his art we will find the same imaginative mode. Characters generally come in pairs. Richard, the *de jure* king, is balanced against Bolingbroke, the *de facto* king; Kent is opposed to Oswald, Ariel to Caliban, Edgar to Edmund. Very often the protagonist is defined by being placed between characters representing opposite poles: Hal between Hotspur, the man of honor and action, and Falstaff; Othello between fiendish Iago and angelic Desdemona; Antony between Cleopatra, the Egyptian, and Octavius, the Roman. This is of course the psychomachia pattern of the moralities—Everyman between Good Angel and

Bad Angel—translated into secular terms. Sometimes the moral absolutism of the early drama is retained, as in *Othello,* and sometimes it is not, as in *Antony and Cleopatra,* where Cleopatra and Octavius do indeed represent, in Rabkin's terms, complementary principles.

Image patterns also come in pairs, clustering around conceptual opposites such as order-chaos, health-disease, music-discord, and so forth. Sometimes the opposed images are used to define a particular situation, like the opposition between sacrifice and butchery in connection with Caesar's murder, and sometimes they become a central structural device, like the suggestive opposition between light and dark in *Othello,* running through the entire play. Very frequently the poetry merely glances at or hints an opposition, as, for example, between Hamlet's unweeded garden that grows to seed and a more innocent garden before his serpent-uncle crept into the orchard with poison in his hand. Imagery merges into locale, and here, too, Shakespeare thinks symmetrically, the forest of Athens balancing the city, Belmont balancing Venice, Arden balancing the court, the tavern world balancing the world of action. The "green worlds" of the comedies have their tragic equivalents in the heaths of *Macbeth* and *Lear,* or in Timon's lonely cave, all opposed to the normal worlds of human intercourse, and of course in *Antony and Cleopatra* the opposition of Egypt and Rome is as obvious and central as white and black in *Othello.*

To some degree all imaginative works are organized symmetrically. We have only to think of the latest novel we have read and probably a pair or two of opposed characters will come to mind. It is even possible that the structure of human thought is such that we consistently organize the world into binary opposites. But to appreciate the significance of Shakespeare's tendency to think in symmetrical patterns we must consider it not only in this large context but in the historical context of Elizabethan culture with its taste for elaborate symmetry in all aspects of art as well as life.

3

Design in Groups of Scenes

Structural Parallels between Scenes

A Shakespearean play is a sequence of individually designed scenes, and there is of course no rule for the number of scenes in a given play. *A Midsummer Night's Dream* has seven, *Antony and Cleopatra* has thirty-six: the number of scenes varies according to Shakespeare's purposes in each play. Between scenes the narrative jumps rather than flows, moving from composition to composition. The story gets told in much the same way that Michelangelo tells the story of the creation and later history in the Sistine ceiling, jumping from crucial and symbolic moment to moment, the first panel showing the division of light from darkness, the second the creation of the sun and moon, the third God separating the waters from the earth, and so forth through the nine biblical panels. Alternatively, we can think of the progression of pageants in the mystery cycles, each pageant play relating an episode in the one great universal history. Or, to pick up again the anachronistic simile I suggested earlier in connection with the presentation of character, we can think of the plays as less like a film with its continuous action than like a photograph album, each composition showing the subject in a different stage of development.

Even as image echoes image in the poetic structure of a play, so scene often echoes scene. We are all more or less familiar with this principle of construction: it is one of Shakespeare's unifying techniques, one of the reasons his plays do not seem merely collections of fragments. In *Troilus and Cressida,* for instance, the

Trojan council (II.ii) is plainly meant to be compared and contrasted with the earlier Greek council (I.iii). In *Romeo and Juliet* the dawn scene in which Romeo leaves Juliet for exile (III.v) echoes the balcony scene in which the lovers exchange vows (II.ii). Excluding the finale in the Capulet tomb, these are the only scenes in which the lovers are alone together. They are also the only scenes to make use of the upper stage, which in this play acquires some symbolic value as a "lofty" place, a kind of ivory tower both transcendent and dangerously removed from common realities. The principle of scenic echoes is familiar: what is not perhaps generally understood is the role that design plays in helping to establish significant parallels between scenes. At times, the repetition of a compositional pattern can be as important as the repetition of an image. Let us look more closely, for example, at the two scenes from *Romeo and Juliet*.

Properly speaking, the balcony "scene" is not a scene at all. Between II.i and II.ii the stage is not cleared, and the two episodes should be considered part of one unit, the fifth scene. This begins with Romeo, who has just come from the Capulet ball, explaining that he is too enamoured to go home: "Can I go forward when my heart is here? / Turn back, dull earth, and find thy centre out" (II.i.1–2). Following his brief soliloquy, Romeo either leaps a property "orchard wall" or withdraws to a conventional hiding place onstage, depending upon how such an action is staged. In any case, he is still onstage when Benvolio and Mercutio enter in high spirits, looking for him.

> *Benvolio.* He ran this way and leapt this orchard wall.
>   Call, good Mercutio.
> *Mercutio.* Nay, I'll conjure too.
>   Romeo! humors! madman! passion! lover!
>   Appear thou in the likeness of a sigh;
>   Speak but one rhyme, and I am satisfied!
>   Cry but 'Ay me!' pronounce but 'love' and 'dove';
>   Speak to my gossip Venus one fair word,
>   One nickname for her purblind son and heir
>   Young Abraham Cupid, he that shot so true
>   When King Cophetua loved the beggar maid!
>   He heareth not, he stirreth not, he moveth not;

> The ape is dead, and I must conjure him.
> I conjure thee by Rosaline's bright eyes,
> By her high forehead and her scarlet lip,
> By her fine foot, straight leg, and quivering thigh,
> And the demesnes that there adjacent lie,
> That in thy likeness thou appear to us!   (II.i.5–21)

Mercutio's irreverent bawdiness sets off the almost religious reverence of the major episode that follows, just as his burlesque conjuring prepares us for the magic of a love that can turn darkness into dawn. The effect of this preliminary segment is to lend Romeo and his passion dignity, for the jests miss their target: Romeo is no longer a mad humorist and Rosaline is not now the name to which he responds.

The lovers' meeting begins with Romeo hailing the dawn:

> But soft! What light through yonder window breaks?
> It is the East, and Juliet is the sun!
> Arise, fair sun, and kill the envious moon,
> Who is already sick and pale with grief
> That thou her maid art far more fair than she.   (II.ii.2–6)

Throughout the episode this imaginary dawn, suggesting the transforming light of love, is played off against the fact that it is night. Romeo and Juliet are alone in a magically transformed world of love's creation that can exist only when the real world is darkened. The real sunrise is feared lest it reveal "all this is but a dream" (II.ii.140). Significantly, toward the end of the balcony episode, the calling motif, established in the Benvolio-Mercutio segment, recurs as the nurse insistently summons Juliet to come in:

> *Nurse.* [*within*] Madam!
> *Juliet.* I come, anon.—But if thou meanest not well,
>   I do beseech thee—
> *Nurse.* [*within*] Madam!
> *Juliet.* By and by I come.   (II.ii.149–152)

In the design of the scene, the lovers are literally surrounded by uncomprehending callers, strangers to their special, transformed world, and these pressures from the impinging outside world help to establish their isolation and perhaps suggest, too, the fragility of their love's creation.

The scene in which Romeo leaves for exile, the fourteenth in the play, is roughly the same length as the fifth scene—they run 232 and 244 lines respectively—and this equivalence, I would judge, is not entirely accidental. Once again the lovers' episode begins at dawn, but this time it is the light of reality rather than love that spreads itself over the scene:

> *Juliet.* Wilt thou be gone? It is not yet near day.
> It was the nightingale, and not the lark,
> That pierced the fearful hollow of thine ear.
> Nightly she sings on yond pomegranate tree.
> Believe me, love, it was the nightingale.
> *Romeo.* It was the lark, the herald of the morn;
> No nightingale. Look, love, what envious streaks
> Do lace the severing clouds in yonder East.
> Night's candles are burnt out, and jocund day
> Stands tiptoe on the misty mountain tops.
> I must be gone and live, or stay and die. (III.v.1-11)

In approximately the middle of the episode the nurse again calls "Madam!" as she did in the balcony episode. This time, however, instead of remaining offstage, she enters, her appearance onstage suggesting that the outside world is forcing its way into the lovers' "dream."

Like the fifth, the fourteenth scene is designed in two segments, a lovers' meeting and an "outsiders" episode. In the fifth scene Romeo was able to hide from Benvolio and Mercutio, but in the fourteenth, after Romeo's departure, Juliet is forced to descend from the upper stage—her descent naturally has symbolic value—and confront first the mother who thinks she weeps for Tybalt, then the father who insists that she marry Paris on Thursday, and finally the nurse, whose only comfort is to assure Juliet that

Romeo is a dishclout compared to Paris. The organization of the fourteenth scene is thus a mirror image of the fifth

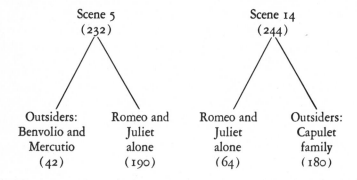

The segments of the fifth scene are arranged to give the effect of the "dream" dominating "reality," the lovers overwhelming the "outsiders" as the short initial segment yields to the long lyric episode. The fourteenth suggests the "dream" dissolving into "day," the magical world of the lovers literally overwhelmed before our eyes.

The *Romeo and Juliet* scenes are widely separated. As we shall see, their placement is important in the overall structure of the play. Very often Shakespeare uses structural parallels of this sort to help articulate his play's design and define the changes that have occurred in the course of the action. Extracted from the body of the play, the two scenes form a "before and after" diptych. Michelangelo's *Fall* comes to mind again as a natural analogy, for here, too, as in the internal design of many scenes, the implicit thought is "Look here upon this picture, and on this."[1]

Structural parallels can be used for other purposes as well Frequently Shakespeare will give us two or three scenes in close. succession designed upon similar patterns in order to produce an effect of intensification through repetition. The fourth and sixth scenes of *Othello* provide a good example. The fourth scene (II.i) shows the arrival of the fleet at Cyprus after the tempest that has driven off the Turks. It begins with Montano and two gentlemen discussing the storm and progressively builds both in intensity and in number of characters onstage as ship after ship arrives safely, first Cassio's, then Iago and Desdemona's, and finally and climactically Othello's:

> O my soul's joy!
> If after every tempest come such calms,
> May the winds blow till they have wakened death!
> And let the laboring bark climb hills of seas
> Olympus-high, and duck again as low
> As hell's from heaven! If it were now to die,
> 'Twere now to be most happy; for I fear
> My soul hath her content so absolute
> That not another comfort like to this
> Succeeds in unknown fate.   (II.i.182–191)

After this triumphant climax the stage is cleared except for Iago, who remains behind to work upon Roderigo and then to soliloquize about his hatred of Othello. The scene as a whole thus falls into two major segments, the crowded arrivals episode, dramatizing a danger safely passed, and the intimate episode in which Iago schemes further against the Moor.

Shakespeare punctuates the end of this scene with the choruslike herald whose proclamation of rejoicing constitutes the fifth scene (II.ii). He then repeats the general pattern of the fourth scene in the night watch (II.iii) in which Iago gets Cassio drunk. Once again the scene's first segment builds in intensity and in number of characters, climaxing with Othello's entrance and his restoration of peace. This second "tempest" passed, the stage is again cleared except for Iago, who remains behind to work upon Cassio and Roderigo in turn.

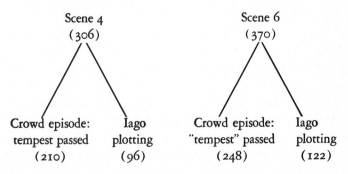

| Scene 4 | | | Scene 6 | |
| (306) | | | (370) | |

Crowd episode:	Iago		Crowd episode:	Iago
tempest passed	plotting		"tempest" passed	plotting
(210)	(96)		(248)	(122)

In each case the pattern of calm after storm is made ironic by the concluding panel devoted to Iago ominously spinning his web. All this section of the play is in fact the calm before the storm: the next major scene is the temptation (III.iii) in which the winds begin to blow in earnest, continuing until they have wakened death.

Liaison between Scenes

The internal design of scenes reveals that structure is as much determined by meaning, by Shakespeare's poetic conceptualization of his material, as it is by purely narrative concerns. The selection of episodes to be dramatized reveals the same interests. Rarely will Shakespeare dramatize an episode for its narrative or theatrical value alone. Indeed, he regularly suppresses or relegates to second-hand report many episodes of considerable narrative, spectacular, or even psychological interest—the murder of the little princes in *Richard III,* for example, or Hamlet's extraordinary attempt to speak with Ophelia in her closet, when he appeared unbraced, ungartered, pale, and with a look "As if he had been loosed out of hell / To speak of horrors" (II.i.83–84). Surely, most modern dramatists would find this episode irresistible.[2]

Especially since Granville-Barker, we have come to understand that Shakespeare's usual practice in relating scene to scene is to select and dispose his material so that each scene comments upon the one preceding. A play is in effect a series of pictures held up for comparison in pairs, first scenes 1 and 2, then 2 and 3, and so forth. In most cases, scenes are presented in roughly chronological order, but the progression of time is by no means regular and steady: Shakespeare will leap over days, months, or even years if necessary to find the next significant moment to hold up before us. These two freedoms, complete freedom of choice in the episodes to be dramatized and almost complete freedom in temporal sequence, allow him to make nearly every scene count.[3]

To a mind accustomed either to a predominantly psychological literary form, like the modern novel, or to a classical style of regular and logical narrative development, the sequence of scenes in a play by Shakespeare is likely to appear capricious and arbitrary. Like the relations between the various episodes within an individual scene, the relations between scenes are often determined by other than narrative concerns, and we will have no difficulty following the logic of a Shakespearean play if we keep this in mind. The temptation scene in *Othello,* for instance, is preceded by the brief and apparently irrelevant scene which shows the Moor on his way to inspect the fortifications of Cyprus (III.ii). An Elizabethan sensibility, accustomed to thinking analogically, would have no difficulty relating this episode to the temptation scene, which reveals how inadequate Othello's personal fortifications are against Iago's siege.

The irony in the case of the fortification and temptation scenes is obvious. Frequently the relations between scenes and the logic behind their ordering is extremely subtle. *Twelfth Night,* for example, opens with a brief scene showing Orsino luxuriating in his unrequited love. Significantly, the duke has not bothered to visit Olivia in person, but has sent Valentine instead. Everything in the scene is contrived to suggest Orsino's inactivity, his lack of vigor, and, appropriately, the scene ends with him departing for his garden to lie voluptuously, like one of Tennyson's lotos-eaters, among the flower beds. The second scene brings on Viola, energetic and vigorous, questioning the captain about Illyria. In the first scene Valentine has described Olivia's emotional self-indulgence: like Orsino luxuriating in his love, Olivia is luxuriating in grief for her dead brother. Viola also fears that she has lost a brother, but instead of watering the beach with tears she resolves to hope for the best and meanwhile makes the practical arrangements necessary for her to live comfortably in a strange country. The order in which these two scenes are presented perhaps seems arbitrary, but if Shakespeare's eye had been principally on the narrative line he probably would have chosen to open the play with the Viola scene, which contains much more in the way of exposition and action than the Orsino scene. I have in fact seen a university production of *Twelfth Night* in which the order of the opening scenes was reversed, presumably to get the action going as quickly as possible. The result was disastrous. Transposed to the opening position, Viola's vigor became unremarkable— we expect a bit of action and exposition in an opening—and lost its point, and so did Orsino's lassitude in consequence of lacking a clear foil.

The third scene of *Twelfth Night* introduces Sir Toby and Sir Andrew and consists mostly of comic foolery at the latter's expense. We have just heard of Olivia's grief and seen the way Viola manages her own sorrow. The third scene picks up the theme of melancholy and bereavement with Toby's opening lines: "What a plague means my niece to take the death of her brother thus? I am sure care's an enemy to life" (I.iii.1–2). The subject of the dead brother is immediately dropped, but the effect of the speech is considerable, for it colors the entire scene, making us see Toby's foolery as the expression of a genuine, if somewhat limited, attitude toward life, one which contrasts with both Orsino's emotionalism and Viola's practicality. Possibly, too, we are meant to see Viola's placement between Orsino and Sir Toby, between excessive melancholy and excessive sanguineness, as significant. Certainly she is in this play a kind of mean between extremes and the character most consistently held up for our admiration.

Toby's "care's an enemy" speech is a signal from the playwright to the audience, who might otherwise miss the relationship between the third scene and the preceding ones. Shakespeare frequently employs such signals when the connection between scenes, the *liaison,* is subtle. Generally, the ligature takes the form of the repetition of a key word or motif from the end of one scene at the beginning of the next. This technique has as its equivalent on the rhetorical level the figure *anadiplosis,* the repetition of a word from one clause at the beginning of the next, as, for instance, in this speech from *Richard III:*

> Come! I have learned that fearful commenting
> Is leaden servitor to dull delay;
> Delay leads impotent and snail-paced beggary. (IV.iii.51–53)

When anadiplosis is continued through a series of clauses the figure is called *climax*. Claudius uses a continued anadiplosis before Hamlet's duel with Laertes:

> Give me the cups,
> And let the kettle to the trumpet speak,
> The trumpet to the cannoneer without,
> The cannons to the heavens, the heaven to earth,
> "Now the king drinks to Hamlet."   (V.ii.263–267)

Here, we may note in passing, the figure is ironically expressive, implying a chain of action and response from earth to heaven and back again, concluding—as the play indeed does—with the king drinking to Hamlet.[4]

It is not unusual in Shakespeare to find a long series of scenes linked, in effect, by continued anadiplosis. Generally he uses the technique when the connection between scenes is conceptual rather than narrative. The first half of *1 Henry IV*, for example, is designed to produce a regular alternation between the "history scenes"—those in which the king and the Percies figure—and the "comedy scenes," concerned with Hal and his disreputable companions. Each scene is thematically related to the preceding one, and, lest we miss the point of the series, Shakespeare provides regular signals to help us follow his thought.

The opening scene of *1 Henry IV* is charged with urgency as Henry and Westmoreland discuss the news from Wales and from the north, Mortimer's capture and Hotspur's victory over the Scots:

> My liege, this haste was hot in question
> And many limits of the charge set down
> But yesternight; when all athwart there came
> A post from Wales, loaden with heavy news.   (I.i.34–37)

Events are happening fast, so fast that the council's decrees of "yesternight" are already out of date. Throughout the scene our attention is repeatedly directed toward the speed with which a dangerous situation is developing, and at the end Henry emphasizes the need for haste:

> Cousin, on Wednesday next our council we
> Will hold at Windsor. So inform the lords;
> But come yourself with speed to us again.   (I.i.103–105)

The second scene introduces the tavern world, picking up precisely where the court scene left off, on the subject of time:

> *Falstaff.*   Now, Hal, what time of day is it, lad?
> *Prince.*   Thou art so fat-witted with drinking of old sack, and unbuttoning thee after supper, and sleeping upon benches after noon, that thou hast forgotten to demand that truly which thou wouldst truly know. What a devil hast thou to do with the time of day? Unless hours were cups of sack, and minutes capons, and clocks the tongues of bawds, and dials the signs of leaping houses, and the blessed sun himself a fair hot wench in flame-colored taffeta, I see no reason why thou shouldst be so superfluous to demand the time of day.   (I.ii.1–11)

A principal point of this scene is the utter temporal disorder in which Falstaff and his companions, "squires of the night's body," live; and the whole scene gravitates toward this theme as Hal and Falstaff make plans to waste time in the Gadshill affair. The scene begins and ends with explicit references to time, Falstaff's question in the one case, and, in the other, Hal's promise to redeem time when men least think he will.

In his soliloquy at the end of the second scene Hal explains that he will imitate the sun, which permits the clouds to hide its face only so that "when he please again to be himself, / Being wanted, he may be more wond'red at" (I.ii.188–189). Hal is saying that eventually he, too, will "be himself." Shakespeare uses this phrase to forge the link with the third scene which begins with King Henry warning the Percies that his patience is wearing thin:

> I will from henceforth rather be myself,
> Mighty and to be feared, than my condition,
> Which hath been smooth as oil, soft as young down.   (I.iii.5–7)

The irony is that, as we know from *Richard II,* it is as much through smoothness as might that Henry won the crown. What is his real nature, his true condition? Is he king or counterfeit? Throughout the first segment of this scene, the confrontation between Henry and the Percies, the issue of his legitimacy is kept implicitly before us. The juxtaposition of the second and third scenes is thus especially suggestive, raising fundamental questions about what it means to "be oneself," asking us to compare the relative honesty of Hal and Henry, and perhaps implying that Hal, even in the tavern, is at least as royal as his father.

The liaison between the third and fourth scenes is clear, and in this case Shakespeare does not need to signal us with the repetition of a phrase. The third scene ends with the Percies discussing their "noble plot"—an ironic adjective surely, for there is something inescapably ignoble about their scheme that reveals itself, as Derek Traversi has suggested,[5] in the language here, in, for example, Worcester's direction to his brother to creep secretly into the archbishop's bosom. The scene's final words are Hotspur's exclamation: "O, let the hours be short / Till fields and blows and groans applaud our sport!" (I.iii.298–299); II.i and II.ii— they may be considered a single scene—show that other plot, the Gadshill robbery, which undercuts the Percies, hinting that perhaps they have something in common with thieves. In fact, in comparison with the "noble plot," the Gadshill affair seems like innocent fun: this, not blows and groans, is sport. However, at the same time that the juxtaposition of scenes 3 and 4 casts the robbery in a relatively favorable light (one reason Shakespeare organized the scenes in this fashion was perhaps to take some of the sting out of a potentially awkward episode), it also keeps before us the plain fact that here is Hal playing at highwayman while elsewhere his enemies are planning to rob him of his crown.

The Gadshill episode ends with Hal and Poins tricking Falstaff by hiding while the robbery is in progress and then rushing out to rob the robbers. The object of the prank is to expose Falstaff's cowardice and have "laughter for a month, and a good jest forever." Yet, merry as it is, the trick reminds us of the adage about no honor amongst thieves, and Shakespeare uses it to provide the liaison with the fifth scene. This begins with Hotspur reading a letter from someone rejecting an invitation to join the Percy conspiracy. The writer suggests that he distrusts the other conspirators, and Hotspur explodes at the imputation that his friends could be unfaithful or his plot ill considered:

What a lackbrain is this! By the Lord, our plot is a good plot as ever was laid; our friends true and constant: a good plot, good friends, and full of expectation; an excellent plot, very good friends. What a frosty-spirited rogue is this! ... Is there not my father, my uncle, and myself; Lord Edmund Mortimer, my Lord of York, and Owen Glendower? Is there not, besides, the Douglas? Have I not all their letters to meet me in arms by the ninth of next month, and are they not some of them set forward already? What a pagan rascal is this! an infidel!   (II.iii.14–27)

But the juxtaposition with the Gadshill affair necessarily colors our attitude toward Hotspur's assertions, and, of course, true and constant are just what the conspirators are not: even Hotspur's father falls prudently ill and proves unfaithful at the crisis.

The first segment of this scene undercuts Hotspur rather severely, suggesting his naiveté; the second, showing the affectionate conversation with his wife, casts him in a more attractive light, revealing that in high spirits he is even capable of a clumsy approach to wit:

> *Lady.*   What is it carries you away?
> *Hotspur.*   Why, my horse, my love—my horse!
> *Lady.*   Out, you mad-headed ape!
>   A weasel hath not such a deal of spleen
>   As you are tossed with. In faith,
>   I'll know your business, Harry; that I will!
>   I fear my brother Mortimer doth stir
>   About his title and hath sent for you
>   To line his enterprise; but if you go—
> *Hotspur.*   So far afoot, I shall be weary, love.
> *Lady.*   Come, come, you paraquito, answer me
>   Directly unto this question that I ask.   (II.iii.72–83)

But, in a play containing Falstaff, it is perhaps more the clumsiness than the wit that strikes us in this exchange. Hotspur is almost painfully single-minded and earnest, qualities not very conducive to wit, and, in the world of this play as in *Hamlet*—Laertes is Hotspur's first cousin—wit has survival value. If Hotspur were a bit less single-minded, he might have understood the skeptical letter-writer's warning. Hotspur's lack of wit provides the liaison with the next scene, the great tavern scene, which, as we remember, begins with the baiting of Francis, another character long on earnestness and short on wit. Lady Percy called Hotspur a "paraquito," and now Hal reflects with astonishment on Francis' having fewer words than a parrot. A moment later the link between the scenes is made secure when Hal mentions Hotspur explicitly, parodying the conversation between Percy and his wife that we have just witnessed.

We can see now that this sequence is more than a series of individual scenes; it is itself a coherent, designed unit, a major segment in the overall structure of the play. The unity of the group is the result not only of the firm thematic connections between scene and scene and the regular, symmetrical alternation between the history and the comedy scenes—this pattern ceases after the tavern scene—but also of the group's consistent focus on a single dominant concern: when is Hal at last going to "be himself," when is he going to assume his place in history? This is the large question that the alternation keeps constantly before us. The movement rises to a climax, as we have seen, in the tavern scene, the turning point of the play. That scene ends with Hal literally and figuratively looking forward to a new dawn, to the morrow when the sun will break through the base contagious clouds that have smothered up his beauty from the world. The next time we see him it is in the interview with his father: he has begun to pay the debt he never promised, and the play's concerns have shifted.

The Scenic Group

The block of related scenes, conceived and designed as a group, is an important structural unit in Shakespeare, an intermediate unit between the scene and the play as a whole. Generally, the group will correspond in some manner to a complete phase in the action or conception of the play. I need hardly warn, however, that the "group" should not be confused with the traditional "act," even though in some cases—for example, the opening group of *Othello,* discussed later in this chapter—the editors, recognizing the coherence of a group of scenes, have marked it off as a separate "act." Frequently a group is formed by an alternating pattern superimposed upon the individual designs of the scenes, as in the *1 Henry IV* series or in the opening series of four scenes in *Hamlet,* which I discuss in the next chapter. In other cases, especially when the component scenes are short and fairly simple in structure, the group will be designed on exactly the same principles as the scene.

As we shall see, an elaborately designed group may at times substitute for a single long scene in the overall design of a play. In the crucial central position of *Lear,* for instance, we find instead of the normal pivotal scene a series of six relatively short scenes conceived and designed as a unit, the storm scenes in which Lear goes mad (III.i-vi).[6] Very often the opening of a play will be a group rather than a single scene. The first three scenes of *Twelfth Night,* for example, are a coherent group. The first and third scenes, devoted to Orsino and Sir Toby respectively, frame, as I suggested earlier, the central scene which introduces Viola, the mean between their extremes: as is often true, extremes meet; both Orsino and Toby represent forms of self-indulgence. Together, the three schematically arranged scenes complete the introduction of the play's themes, which is the normal function of an opening scene in Shakespeare. The fourth scene, in which Orsino instructs Viola to woo Olivia for him, begins a new phase, starting the action proper.

A similar group opens *Richard II.* Here the two formal, ceremonial scenes devoted to the chivalric contest between Bolingbroke and Mowbray (I.i and I.iii) frame the intimate conversation between Gaunt and his sister (I.ii) in which Shakespeare reveals the reality behind Richard's public display of impartial justice, that is, the fact that Richard himself is responsible for Gloucester's death.

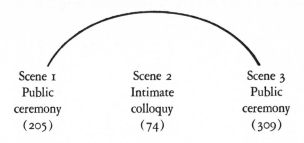

Scene 1	Scene 2	Scene 3
Public	Intimate	Public
ceremony	colloquy	ceremony
(205)	(74)	(309)

Unified by the almost continuous presence onstage of "time-honored Lancaster," the embodiment of England's noble past, the opening group is designed to introduce us to a world in which public appearances are to be distrusted, a world that has lost the innocent frankness that Gaunt symbolizes. Shakespeare is feeling his way toward *Hamlet* and also toward *Lear,* for this group can be seen as the forerunner of the great *Lear* opening with its analogous contrast between public and private. Like Lear, Richard is fundamentally confused about the distinction between the two spheres: he has so little sense of himself as a man as well as a king that without the title he becomes in his own eyes "nothing," a nameless, faceless ghost of his former self. Unable to define his position in the world, Richard lapses into madness or near-madness. Shakespeare carries the logic of the situation further in the later play—Lear discovers a new identity in his common humanity —but in theme the two plays are similar, and in each case the opening is designed to establish the distinction between public and private and thus to draw our attention to the protagonist's problems.

Usually Shakespeare's reasons for opening with a group instead of a single scene are obvious: in *Twelfth Night,* and perhaps *Richard II* as well, the dramatic material simply does not lend itself to a single big scene. *Macbeth,* however, might very well have opened with a major scene, a large court scene, perhaps, in which Duncan's hieratic sanctity would be established as he invested Macbeth with his new title. In fact the play opens with a sequence of seven brief scenes, designed as a group and leading to the first big scene, the murder discussed in the last chapter. Possibly the choice in this case was for dramatic effect. The series of brief scenes produces the effect of a headlong rush of events with little leisure for reflection: we are shocked by the speed with which we arrive at the murder itself, but, this point reached, Shakespeare gives us the extended murder scene, drawing out the nightmarish implications of the situation to which the rush has brought us. In other words, the pacing contrives to recreate in the audience something like the murderer's own experience.

The *Macbeth* group is unusually complex. The first scene, introducing the witches, serves as prologue to the group and the play. This is followed by two subgroups of three scenes each—the first series located somewhere in the open fields, the second in Macbeth's castle. Each subgroup is designed as if it were an individual scene, the first principally concerned with Macbeth and the second with Lady Macbeth. For the sake of clarity, it is perhaps best to approach this series with a diagram of the overall pattern in mind.

Prologue: Fields: Castle:

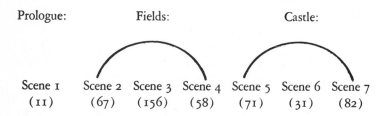

Scene 1 Scene 2 Scene 3 Scene 4 Scene 5 Scene 6 Scene 7
(11) (67) (156) (58) (71) (31) (82)

The opening of a Shakespeare play, as we have seen, normally establishes a bold opposition between two themes, motifs, or even worlds—hate and love in *Romeo and Juliet* or the court and tavern perspectives on life in *1 Henry IV*. Much of the drama, at any rate in the early phases of the play, comes from the conflict implicit in this opposition. The drama of "ideas"—the term is of course only approximate—is as important as the drama of action. In *Richard II* Shakespeare shows us the world of public surfaces before revealing, in the second scene, the underlying reality. In

Macbeth, as in *Hamlet,* he reverses the procedure, intensifying the irony and the drama. The witches' prologue introduces us immediately to the mysterious, frightening world of evil. The second scene brings us the public surface, the normal world of traitors and battles, but we are aware now that there is more to this world than meets the eye. Nearly every line in this short scene seems ominously foreboding, from Duncan's simple question, "What bloody man is that?" (I.ii.1) to the echo of the prologue as the mantle of the traitor Cawdor passes to Macbeth: "What he hath lost noble Macbeth hath won" (I.ii.67).

The second scene is balanced by the fourth, which is roughly equivalent in length and in which Duncan again figures prominently. The king hears of Cawdor's execution, remarking

> There's no art
> To find the mind's construction in the face.
> He was a gentleman on whom I built
> An absolute trust.   (I.iv.11–14)

Immediately, Macbeth enters and Duncan embraces him with absolute trust:

> Welcome hither:
> ⌐ have begun to plant thee and will labor
> To make thee full of growing.   (I.iv.27–29)

Once again we are in the world of normal surfaces and once again our special knowledge gives nearly every speech an ironic ring. Placed in the emphatic central position, framed by the two brief Duncan scenes concerned with the normal face of things, is the crucial third scene in which Macbeth meets the witches and begins to meditate murder.

The field series—scenes 2, 3, and 4—can perhaps be understood as analogous in structure and function to the usual big opening scene. Together the three scenes run nearly 300 lines, roughly the same length as the *Lear* opening or the second scene —the opening scene proper—of *Hamlet.* The group introduces and "places" the protagonist, and establishes the opposition between public surfaces and the mysterious, working mind of evil. The castle series—scenes 5, 6, and 7—which is somewhat shorter, can be understood as analogous to the usual second scene. The scenes that follow the openings in *Hamlet* and *Lear* focus on the Polonius and Gloucester families respectively, relatively simple characters who serve as foils to the more complex protagonists. The castle series introduces and focuses on Lady Macbeth, who embraces evil with so much more enthusiasm than her husband. Attempting to do justice to her complexity, we might say that Lady Macbeth willfully makes herself more simple in response than Macbeth.

The design of the castle series is the reverse of the field series. Instead of two public scenes framing a centerpiece concerned with hidden evil, we have two private scenes framing a public centerpiece—the sixth scene, in which Lady Macbeth welcomes Duncan to her house. The relative proportions of the component scenes are also changed; this time the centerpiece is the briefest unit in the series. The effect of these changes, like that of the shift from the open air to the interior of the castle, is perhaps to give us a sense of penetrating deeper into an inner world. Alternatively, we can say that Shakespeare begins the play with a major composition, the field series, in which the image of Macbeth rapt in thought as he confronts the witches is significantly placed between two public panels: the design symbolizes his situation. The second composition, the castle series, is also expressive, showing Duncan hemmed in, circumscribed, by the husband and wife plotting to murder him.

The fifth and seventh scenes, the two side panels of the castle series, are parallel in design. The fifth scene begins with Lady Macbeth alone in meditation, reading the letter in which Macbeth describes the witches and their prophecy. The scene's second segment gives us the brief interview in which Lady Macbeth begins to exert pressure upon her husband. The seventh scene also has two segments, a monologue and an interview. This time we begin with Macbeth in soliloquy, considering the murder—"If it were done when 'tis done, then 'twere well / It were done quickly"

(I.vii.1–2)—after which Lady Macbeth enters and heaps scorn on her husband for his fears.

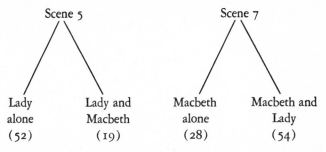

Scene 5		Scene 7	
Lady alone	Lady and Macbeth	Macbeth alone	Macbeth and Lady
(52)	(19)	(28)	(54)

The lengths of the various segments are important. Scene 5 begins with a long and exceptionally fierce segment, followed by the brief conversation in which Macbeth seems doubtful about the murder. Scene 7 begins with a brief segment in which Macbeth further explores his doubts, after which Lady Macbeth in the long final segment chides him for not being sufficiently manly, proclaiming that rather than not kill Duncan she would murder her own child:

> I have given suck, and know
> How tender 'tis to love the babe that milks me:
> I would, while it was smiling in my face,
> Have plucked my nipple from his boneless gums
> And dashed the brains out, had I so sworn as you
> Have done to this.   (I.vii.54–59)

The effect of the design, then, is to show Macbeth's relative decency overwhelmed and circumscribed by his wife's ferocity. Just as Duncan is surrounded by his treacherous hosts, so Macbeth himself is enveloped by savagery.

Superimposed on the separate designs of the two subgroups, the field scenes and the castle scenes, is a regular pattern of alternation between scenes concerned with evil's hidden workings and ironic public scenes concerned with the appearance of normality. Beginning with the prologue, we have in turn the witches, Duncan hearing reports of victories, Macbeth meeting the witches, Duncan receiving Macbeth, Lady Macbeth alone and with her husband, Lady Macbeth receiving Duncan, and finally Macbeth alone and with his wife. Moreover, alternate scenes are designed to echo each other:

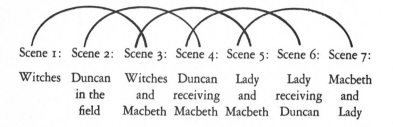

Scene 1:	Scene 2:	Scene 3:	Scene 4:	Scene 5:	Scene 6:	Scene 7:
Witches	Duncan in the field	Witches and Macbeth	Duncan receiving Macbeth	Lady and Macbeth	Lady receiving Duncan	Macbeth and Lady

The nature of the correspondence is clear in every case except perhaps one, the third and fifth scenes. The third scene opens with the witches alone, after which Macbeth enters and they hail him by his various titles. The fifth scene opens with Lady Macbeth alone, practicing witchcraft:

> Come you spirits
> That tend on mortal thoughts, unsex me here,
> And fill me from the crown to the toe top-full
> Of direst cruelty.   (I.v.38–41)

And when Macbeth enters, she, too, hails him by his titles: "Great Glamis! worthy Cawdor! / Greater than both, by the all-hail hereafter!" (I.v.52–53). Shakespeare is asking us to see Lady Macbeth as the mortal equivalent of the weird sisters.

The Othello Group

Generally, scenes organized into groups retain their independence and can be analyzed either individually or as parts of larger structures. In a few cases, however, a series is melded so completely that the individual scenes become relatively unimportant as units of design. The moonlit, enchanted atmosphere of the long forest centerpiece in *A Midsummer Night's Dream,* for example, is so powerful that the unit gives, and was plainly intended to give, the impression of a single continuous action. The forest sequence is traditionally divided into five scenes; actually there are only three—the third (II.i), fourth (II.ii and III.i), and fifth (III.ii and IV.i) of the play.⁷ We can, if we wish, analyze these scenes individually; they reveal the normal principles of design. But the functional unit in the overall structure of the play is the group as a whole.

The first three scenes of *Othello* are so closely knit that after a performance or reading it is difficult even to recall that they are separate scenes; the edges melt and we remember only a single long movement, the Venice action, clearly distinguished from the rest of the play, which is set in Cyprus. More important than place, however, which on Shakespeare's stage cannot be visually realized, the three scenes share a special, symbolic nighttime atmosphere visually realized in the use of torches throughout the central section of the group.

The three scenes together run nearly 700 lines, and as a group they serve in lieu of one long opening scene. The first shows Iago and Roderigo rousing Brabantio with news of Desdemona's elopement. In the second Brabantio confronts Othello in the streets. The third is the council scene in which Brabantio and Othello put their cases before the duke, who decides in favor of Othello, dispatching him to defend Cyprus from the advancing Turks.

The first thing to notice is that the group begins and ends with the focus on Iago. The opening segment is a conversation between Iago and Roderigo. Roderigo complains that Iago has treated him unfairly in not telling him about Desdemona's marriage, to which Iago replies that he knew nothing of it, assuring Roderigo that he hates Othello for promoting Cassio rather than himself. This segment has its counterpart at the end of the group in a second Iago-Roderigo colloquy in which Iago ridicules Roderigo's romantic despair and indeed the whole notion of romantic love:

If the balance of our lives had not one scale of reason to poise another of sensuality, the blood and baseness of our natures would conduct us to most preposterous conclusions. But we have reason to cool our raging motions, our carnal stings, our unbitted lusts; whereof I take this that you call love to be a sect or scion.   (I.iii.326–331)

Once again Iago assures Roderigo that he hates Othello, packing the gull off to sell his estate for money with which to woo Desdemona. A brief coda follows, the soliloquy in which Iago reveals that he is using Roderigo for his own purposes. Iago's goal is revenge, but, surprisingly, his motive no longer seems to be Cassio's preferment, but the suspicion that Othello has cuckolded him: "I know not if't be true; / But I, for mere suspicion in that kind, / Will do as if for surety" (I.iii.382–384). At the very end of the group Iago announces that he has a plot: "I have't! It is engend'red! Hell and night / Must bring this monstrous birth to the world's light" (I.iii.397–398). The rhyme-words "night" and "light" summarize the basic opposition of motifs which the group establishes.

By having Iago speak in terms of engendering, Shakespeare ironically emphasizes his barren destructiveness. Hate and love, suggestively associated with night and light, are one set of antitheses introduced in this opening group, which is designed so that the Iago segments circumscribe the long centerpiece in which Othello and Desdemona's love is directly presented. Significantly, there are no torches onstage in the side panels, whereas the centerpiece is almost continually torchlit. The overall composition is thus an emblem of the way love is destroyed by hate in this play, of the way light is surrounded by darkness.[8]

Let us look more closely at the centerpiece, which is a diptych, the two panels running 208 and 300 lines respectively.

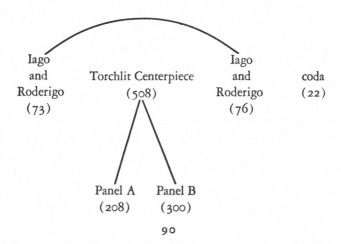

The first panel consists of a series of urgent, impassioned, torchlit comings and goings, climaxing in the direct confrontation between Brabantio and Othello. It begins with Iago bidding Roderigo to wake Brabantio "with like timorous accent and dire yell / As when, by night and negligence, the fire / Is spied in populous cities" (I.i.75–77). In fact, Iago is not announcing a fire, he is kindling one, rousing Brabantio's fury as he will later rouse Othello's. He plays upon Brabantio's fears, vividly describing Desdemona and Othello in sexual embrace until the man is thoroughly distraught.

> Strike on the tinder, ho!
> Give me a taper! Call up all my people!
> This accident is not unlike my dream.
> Belief of it oppresses me already.
> Light, I say! light!   (I.i.139–143)

Accompanied by torchbearers, the impassioned father makes a brief appearance on the main stage, calls for weapons, and then hurries off in search of the Moor. Almost immediately Othello and Iago enter, also accompanied by torchbearers, Iago pretending to be furious at the outrage to his master: "Nine or ten times / I had thought t'have yerked him here under the ribs" (I.ii.4–5). Next Cassio, bringing more torchbearers, summons Othello to the council, and Shakespeare weaves him into the dominant mood by having him excitedly insist on the urgency of the duke's business, and into the dominant image of a growing, spreading fire by having him speak of the matter as "of some heat" and Othello "hotly called for" (I.ii.40, 44). Finally, Brabantio and his attendants return—there are now three separate parties of torchbearers onstage—and the irate father accuses Othello of bewitching his daughter. Through all this impassioned activity Othello maintains perfect self-control, refusing to allow Iago to arouse his anger, calmly inquiring about the state business, and meeting Brabantio with reasonableness and respect: "Keep up your bright swords, for the dew will rust them. / Good signior, you shall more command with years / Than with your weapons" (I.ii.59–61).

The division between the two panels is punctuated by the

rhymed couplet at the end of I.ii. (There is no punctuating couplet at the end of I.i, between Brabantio's exit and Othello's entrance with Iago.) Moreover, just as there is an expressive distinction in visual effect between the "dark" Iago frame and the torchlit centerpiece, so there is a distinction between the two panels of the centerpiece. In the first the torches, which become associated with passion, are in continual movement. In the second the lights are stationary and a significant tableau is formed, the council table flanked by torchbearers providing an emblem of authority and reason.[9] The movement of the centerpiece, from the rousing of passion in the first panel to final judgment in the second, reflects in miniature the larger pattern of the play—the rousing of Othello's jealousy, which leads to the stern judgment he executes first upon Desdemona and then upon himself in the finale.

The second panel of the centerpiece begins with the council considering various reports of Turkish naval movements.

> *Duke.* There is no composition in these news
>   That gives them credit.
> *1 Senator.* Indeed they are disproportioned.
>   My letters say a hundred and seven galleys.
> *Duke.* And mine a hundred forty.
> *2 Senator.* And mine two hundred.
>   But though they jump not on a just account—
>   As in these cases where the aim reports
>   'Tis oft with difference—yet do they all confirm
>   A Turkish fleet, and bearing up to Cyprus.   (I.iii.1–8)

There is a subtle analogy between the opening of this panel and that of the previous one: in each case an authority—Brabantio, the Venetian council—is roused in the middle of the night to deal with confusing reports of a barbarian's assaults on a precious dependent. (Later in the council scene Brabantio explicitly compares his case to the state's.) But whereas Brabantio is impassioned, the council deals with its problem with conspicuous calm. The dramatic contrast between the two centerpiece panels establishes the antithesis of passion and reason, which functions in this play in a manner not entirely unlike the way the public-private antithesis functions in *Lear*. In the first panel Othello's rationality strikes us by its contrast with the other characters' excitement; in the second Brabantio's passion stands out. Once again Brabantio accuses Othello of witchcraft:

> She is abused, stol'n from me, and corrupted
> By spells and medicine bought of mountebanks;
> For nature so prepost'rously to err,
> Being not deficient, blind, or lame of sense,
> Sans witchcraft could not.   (I.iii.60–64)

We should not underestimate, I think, the fact that this strange union between a black general and a Venetian lady is, at face value, "unnatural." Brabantio's conviction that his daughter must be blind or lame of sense has weight, although not perhaps in exactly the way he means.

In reply Othello undertakes to prove with "a round unvarnished tale" that he used no magic, that Desdemona's love for him is only reasonable. The "proof" is the long speech in which he describes how Desdemona listened tearfully to his adventures:

> She loved me for the dangers I had passed,
> And I loved her that she did pity them.
> This only is the witchcraft I have used.   (I.iii.167–169)

The duke finds Othello's argument convincing: "I think this tale would win my daughter too" (I.iii.171), he says, advising Brabantio to yield. But the duke's opinion is not necessarily meant to be the last word. There is tragic irony, I think, in Othello's confidence that there was no magic involved in winning Desdemona, that their love is wholly reasonable. Love in Shakespeare is always a kind of witchcraft, something ultimately inexplicable in rational terms. (We recall, for instance, Demetrius and Lysander's absurd conviction that their passions are reasonable.) There is as much magic in the web of Othello and Desdemona's union as there is in the handkerchief that symbolizes it. Othello's confusion about the nature of love, analogous to Lear's confusion, is important: his ignorance of the irrational side of human nature helps make him vulnerable to Iago's scheme, for, once his suspicions are aroused, it does seem plausible to him that Desdemona might be unfaithful. Characteristically, Othello seeks rational proof of Desdemona's love—or rather, her lack of love:

> Make me to see't; or at the least so prove it
> That the probation bear no hinge nor loop
> To hang a doubt on—or woe upon thy life!
> (III.iii.364–366)

In matters of faith—as many have noticed, the play has religious overtones—reliance upon reason alone, demands for "ocular proof" of spiritual realities, can lead one to deny the obvious.

Let us return for a moment to the outer panels in this group of scenes, the Iago-Roderigo conversations. Iago supposes himself an eminently reasonable man, able to manipulate gulls like Roderigo precisely because he is not subject to their "raging motions." Yet in his hate Iago is as passionate as any lover. The much-debated subject of Iago's motivation, including the issue of whether the concept of motivation is even appropriate in this case, lies beyond the scope of my discussion. It seems to me at least possible, however, that we are expected to observe that the reasons Iago offers for his hate in the coda, the closing soliloquy, are no more adequate than the reasons Othello offers for his and Desdemona's love. Hatred is as irrational—and consequently as finally mysterious—as love: Iago is the fiendish opposite of Desdemona. At first he also appears the complete opposite of Othello's free and open spirit, but the contrast is not without a touch of irony. Equally confused about their natures, Iago and Othello are made for mutual destruction. Nor is the design of the group, the contrast between the darkness of the frame and the light of the centerpiece, without irony: among other things, the torches illuminate the inescapable blackness of Othello's skin.[10]

4

The Design of *Hamlet*

The approach to Shakespearean structure in terms of "multiple unity"—that is, regarding the play as a sequence of relatively independent units, each a composition, a speaking picture, in its own right—can significantly alter the way we "see" Shakespeare's plays. It does not, or at any rate it need not, lead us to alter our generally accepted interpretations. But it can help us to follow the structural emphases built into the plays, and thus to relate our interpretations much more firmly to the concrete dramatic artifacts before us. It can be especially useful in the classroom because it anchors discussion to a manageable yet rich dramatic unit. Close analysis of the imagery and organization of individual speeches can give students a sense of Shakespeare as a poet but not as a playwright. Ideally, close analysis of scenes, paying attention to nonverbal as well as verbal elements, can give them both.

We are all aware of the importance of context in literary interpretation. Take a phrase, or an episode, out of context and it changes color, becoming capable of many readings plainly impossible *in situ.* On the other hand, even a relatively colorless incident, like Hal correcting the sheriff about the time of day at the end of the tavern scene—"I think it is good morrow, is it not?" (II.iv.500)—acquires a certain resonance in context. In Shakespeare studies we usually take account of the immediate dramatic context and the larger context of the play as a whole, the "world" of the play. We examine the plays with a microscope and a telescope by turns. Scenic analysis can, I think, expand our sense of context in Shakespeare by directing our attention to the actual units in which the plays are designed. In order to suggest how this approach can be applied to an entire play, I shall go through *Hamlet* scene by scene, sketching at least in outline the way each scene is constructed.

1. The Prologue (I.i)

Structurally, the first scene, in which neither Hamlet nor Claudius appears, functions as a prologue. In fact, the scene calls attention to its own function when Horatio recalls the death of Julius Caesar, remarking that before that calamity, too, ghosts and ill omens served as a prologue to the fearful events coming on. Much has been written about the suggestiveness of the ominous battlements scene, about the way it establishes the dark coloring and mysterious "interrogative mood" of the play.[1] Less familiar is the scene's design.

The prologue falls into five segments, its structure defined by the ghost's two appearances. The preliminary segment is the changing of the guard, running 39 lines. This concludes with Horatio sitting down to hear from Bernardo about the ghost:

> Sit down awhile,
> And let us once again assail your ears,
> That are so fortified against our story,
> What we two nights have seen.   (30–33)

The lines signal the audience to expect a formal expository speech, but almost immediately the ghost enters, making description superfluous. The ghost segment runs 12 lines, after which Bernardo and Marcellus sit down to hear Horatio's description of King Hamlet's single combat with Fortinbras. This is the real expository speech, and it, too, is signaled in advance:

> Good now, sit down, and tell me he that knows,
> Why this same strict and most observant watch
> So nightly toils the subject of the land.   (70–72)

Shakespeare's device here of catching the audience up short with a false signal and a sudden surprise, the ghost, is of course sound dramatic technique, the kind of thing any good playwright or novelist learns to do in order to stimulate interest. The feint reinforces our sense of the uncertainty of this play's world, and, equally important, it helps to throw extra emphasis on the real expository speech, which comes, in effect, twice telegraphed. It also helps shift the scene's focus from the simple fact of the ghost to its significance, for Horatio answers Marcellus' question about the strict watch indirectly at first, going back to the single-combat, which may be taken as the play's primal image and point of departure.

The expository episode in which Marcellus and Bernardo listen to Horatio is emphasized in other ways as well. At 74 lines it is by far the scene's longest segment. Moreover, it occupies the central position, framed by the two, roughly equal, appearances of the ghost and the opening and concluding segments, again roughly equal:

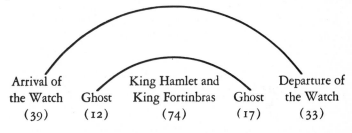

| Arrival of the Watch (39) | Ghost (12) | King Hamlet and King Fortinbras (74) | Ghost (17) | Departure of the Watch (33) |

Thinking purely in narrative terms, the fight between the kings is not worth the kind of emphasis that we would expect to find reserved for the crucial fact at the heart of the story—that Claudius murdered Hamlet. Again, thinking in narrative terms, we might be tempted to suppose that the centerpiece of this scene is a second feint, for after all the play is only tangentially concerned with the fortunes of the Norwegian dynasty. We recall, however, that it is often a conceptual rather than a narrative element that Shakespeare places in the center of his scenes, sometimes a direct statement such as Kent's warning to the king to "see better" in the center of the opening scene of *Lear,* and sometimes a rich emblem such as the porter's evocation of hell in the center of the *Macbeth* murder scene.

The image of Hamlet and Fortinbras face to face in a royal combat ratified by law and heraldry, thus emphatically placed in the prologue, persists throughout the play as the symbol of all that is noble and irretrievable, all that Claudius permanently poisoned when serpent-like he crept into the garden. The memory of the two valiant kings haunts the tragedy, looming behind each pass of the incensed points of the modern mighty opposites, Hamlet and his uncle, and looming also behind the final combat, Hamlet and Laertes' poisoned play, swaddled in a show of chivalry as "yeasty" as the eloquence of Osric, the waterfly who presides as master of the lists. But of course the picture that Horatio paints in the center of this scene is already elegiac, an image of a falling-off rather than a simple evocation of the ideal. Both kings are dead, and the new Fortinbras is as brutal and lawless as he is bold: it is his repudiation of the chivalric compact that has given rise to Danish fears of invasion.

No sooner has Horatio finished his description of young Fortinbras and compared the present state of Denmark to that of ill-omened Rome than the ghost, as if to confirm the death of chivalry, reappears, only to flee almost immediately as the cock crows. Dawn is always significant in Shakespeare. Normally it has connotations of truth coming to light—as in the *1 Henry IV* tavern scene, the *Macbeth* murder scene, or the second lovers' scene of *Romeo and Juliet*—and so it does here, for the ghost is a fact about which young Hamlet must be informed. But the sunrise also brings us to the false brightness of the court, the seeming glow of confidence and health as an able king dispatches his business.

2. The Opening Scene (I.ii)

At the conclusion of the prologue we may imagine a short pause in which the stage remains empty to punctuate the completion of the initial composition, after which the trumpets sound a

flourish and the glittering court figures, gorgeously costumed, perhaps as many as 20 or 25 actors and extras in all, ceremoniously
enter. Claudius, naturally, takes center stage with Gertrude at his
side, the others disposi g emselves symmetrically about him to
form the usual court tableau. The bold juxtaposition of this bright
picture with the black prologue is an example of Shakespeare's
mature technique at its finest. Not every element in the tableau
is bright, however; Hamlet wears the "nighted color" of deep
mourning, visually recalling the first scene and suggesting that the
worlds of darkness and daylight, seemingly dissociated, are perhaps intimately related. Moreover, to link this scene with the prologue, Shakespeare, with heavy irony, has Claudius' first words
refer to the dead king: "Though yet of Hamlet our dear brother's
death / The memory be green" (1–2), he begins, declaring in
effect that the former king's reign is a closed book.

The long second scene introduces the major characters and
opens the play proper. Like most of Shakespeare's opening scenes
it is highly organized. It begins with the court episode, running
128 lines, in which Claudius neatly ticks off, point by point, his
business of the day, first disposing of the former king, next dispatching Cornelius and Voltemand to Norway, then consenting to
Laertes' request to go to France, and finally denying Hamlet's
request to return to Wittenberg. Each character, as his case is
taken up, evidently advances and stands before the king, and we
should notice that it is exactly midway in the segment that Claudius turns to Hamlet: "But now, my cousin Hamlet, and my son"
(64). The prince, who until this moment has probably been
standing well to one side, steps forward, bringing the darkness of
the battlements scene back to center stage in immediate juxtaposition with the king.

Implicit throughout the prologue was the image of a citadel be-
seiged, and this motif of encirclement is echoed now as it gradually becomes apparent that Hamlet is imprisoned in Denmark,
a court and a world that he loathes. Hamlet thought to flee to
Wittenberg, but Claudius will not allow him out of sight, and the
court episode ends with the king announcing that he will celebrate

Hamlet's "gentle and unforced" yielding on this point by firing his cannon to the heavens. One other more desperate route of escape still seems open to the prince, and as soon as the stage is cleared he considers the possibility of this course, suicide, only to remind himelf that against this stands another sort of "canon," one fixed by God. On either side the road from Elsinore is guarded, and all that remains to Hamlet is his disgust for the world and the feeble wish that somehow his flesh will of itself melt into a puddle.

Hamlet's cannon pun provides the liaison between the court segment and the centerpiece, the "too too sullied flesh" soliloquy. Whatever else may be said about it, the main thrust of this soliloquy is the vivid contrast Hamlet draws between his father and Claudius—"So excellent a king, that was to this / Hyperion to a satyr" (139–140)—and his outrage at Gertrude's inability to perceive the difference between the two. In Hamlet's eyes, his mother's essential failing is her moral blindness, a defect made evident by the wicked speed with which she rushed into an incestuous second marriage. Like the centerpiece of the prologue, the central panel of this scene is an image of a great falling-off from a heroic, specifically a godlike, past.

The "too too sullied flesh" soliloquy, fiercely painting the contrast between King Claudius and King Hamlet, is the pivot on which the scene as a whole turns. The first segment, the court episode, presented Claudius for our consideration. The final segment, balancing the first, is concerned with King Hamlet. Horatio, Marcellus, and Bernardo enter, and very soon the conversation turns to the late king:

> *Hamlet.* My father—methinks I see my father.
> *Horatio.* Where, my lord?
> *Hamlet.* In my mind's eye, Horatio.
> *Horatio.* I saw him once. 'A was a goodly king.
> *Hamlet.* 'A was a man, take him for all in all,
> I shall not look upon his like again.
> *Horatio.* My lord, I think I saw him yesternight. (184–189)

The emphasis on seeing here is, under the circumstances, tensely dramatic. It also helps to evoke in our mind's eye a vivid image so that when Horatio describes in detail the ghost's appearance, "Armed at point exactly, cap-a-pe" (200), we too see King Hamlet again and can compare his grave, martial figure with that of the smiling politician of the court episode, the cautious, crafty man whose most congenial instrument is a go-between. The scene as a whole thus resolves itself into a triptych with a Claudius panel on one side and a King Hamlet panel on the other, the prince significantly placed in the middle.

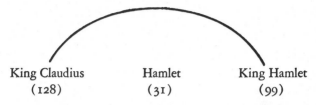

King Claudius   Hamlet   King Hamlet
(128)   (31)   (99)

We are reminded of the way Othello is circumscribed by Iago in the Venice scenes. So Hamlet is circumscribed, trapped between the present and the past, between the reality of his uncle and the ideal of his father.

3. *The Polonii (I.iii)*

If the third scene opened the play, we would probably take the remarks of Polonius and his children at face value. Certainly we would be less inclined to disparage the very sensible maxims Polonius loads upon his son. But our angle of approach is determined by the final segment of the preceding scene. We understand already that there are more things in heaven and earth than conventional wisdom comprehends, and we perceive the intellectual limitations of the Polonii very clearly. Hamlet is circumscribed by his uncle and his father placed on either side; the Polonii are defined by having their scene placed between two episodes concerned with the ghost.

Nominally, it is Laertes who is the "free" man, and the scene begins with an affirmation of his liberty as he informs his sister that his "necessaries are embarked" and himself about to sail for France. A moment later Laertes speaks of Hamlet's lack of freedom, warning Ophelia that the prince's "will is not his own":

> For he himself is subject to his birth.
> He may not, as unvalued persons do,
> Carve for himself, for on his choice depends
> The safety and health of this whole state,
> And therefore must his choice be circumscribed
> Unto the voice and yielding of that body
> Whereof he is the head.   (17–24)

One of Shakespeare's basic strategies in this scene is to have Laertes and Polonius say more than they understand. Here Laertes means simply that Hamlet as heir apparent may not be free to marry Ophelia, but in a larger sense, too, Hamlet is "subject to his birth," bound by being the dead king's son, and upon his "carving" —his rapier and dagger-work—the safety and health of Denmark literally depend.

Like the preceding scene, this one falls into three segments: first Laertes gives advice to Ophelia (51 lines); then Polonius gives advice to Laertes (36 lines); finally Polonius gives advice to Ophelia (49 lines). Although significantly different in imagery, both the brother's and the father's warnings about Hamlet are much the same in substance, and Polonius, too, touches upon the subject of Hamlet's freedom when he remarks that the prince may walk with a "larger tether" than Ophelia: larger in some respects it may be, but it is a tether still.

Framed by the parallel Ophelia segments, the advice to Laertes occupies the emphatic central position in the scene.

>   Give thy thoughts no tongue,
> Nor any unproportioned thought his act.
> Be thou familiar, but by no means vulgar.
> Those friends thou hast, and their adoption tried,
> Grapple them unto thy soul with hoops of steel,
> But do not dull thy palm with entertainment
> Of each new-hatched, unfledged courage. Beware
> Of entrance to a quarrel; but being in,
> Bear't that th'opposed may beware of thee.
> Give every man thine ear, but few thy voice;
> Take each man's censure, but reserve thy judgment.
> Costly thy habit as thy purse can buy,
> But not expressed in fancy; rich, not gaudy,

For the apparel oft proclaims the man,
And they in France of the best rank and station
Are of a most select and generous chief in that.
Neither a borrower nor a lender be,
For loan oft loses both itself and friend,
And borrowing dulleth edge of husbandry.
This above all, to thine own self be true,
And it must follow as the night the day
Thou canst not then be false to any man.   (59–80)

Point for point, Polonius unwittingly describes the precepts according to which Hamlet will cautiously proceed, keeping his thoughts to himself, avoiding rash action, grappling his one tried friend to his soul, and, above all, attempting to remain true to himself. It has often been noted that Polonius "recks not his own rede," in particular, when he jumps to rash conclusions about the cause of Hamlet's madness. Perhaps equally important, Laertes, who is like Hamlet to be a revenger, point for point violates his father's maxims, rashly bursting into the king's presence to bellow out his rage, unwisely trusting Claudius, and, above all, being false to his fundamental decency and Hamlet's by stooping to the treachery of a poisoned foil.

4. The Ghost Scene (I.iv-v)[2]

After the oppressive complacency of the third scene, we find ourselves back in the night world for Hamlet's confrontation with the ghost. In comparison with Polonius' constricted sphere, Hamlet's world seems, ironically, spacious, and the prince's opening line, "The air bites shrewdly; it is very cold," gives us a sense of the freedom of the open air, as well as a hint of hostility in the environment. Almost immediately, however, we are reminded of Hamlet's jailer, the offstage flourish and cannon discharge recalling Claudius' promise to fire his cannon to celebrate Hamlet's remaining in Elsinore.

The sound of the king's cannon leads to Hamlet's discussion of the notorious Danish custom of "heavy-headed revel" and the comparison of national faults with the particular flaws of individuals:

> So oft it chances in particular men
> That (for some vicious mole of nature in them,
> As in their birth, wherein they are not guilty,
> Since nature cannot choose his origin)
> By the o'ergrowth of some complexion,
> Oft breaking down the pales and forts of reason,
> Or by some habit that too much o'erleavens
> The form of plausive manners—that (these men
> Carrying, I say, the stamp of one defect,
> Being nature's livery, or fortune's star)
> Their virtues else, be they as pure as grace,
> As infinite as man may undergo,
> Shall in the general censure take corruption
> From that particular fault. The dram of evil
> Doth all the noble substance of a doubt,
> To his own scandal.   (I.iv.22–38)

This is one of the knottiest passages in the play, and it is probably textually corrupt as well. Whether Hamlet is talking about his own melancholy is uncertain, but we are secure, I think, in noting that the speech echoes Laertes' remark about Hamlet's being subject to his birth, and that the dominant image is the picture of a sound body progressively corrupted by a dram of evil. Whatever else it may be, this passage is a prologue to the ghost's appearance. No sooner is Hamlet finished than his father, physically corrupted by Claudius' poison, enters and tethers the prince to the responsibility of his birth. "Speak," Hamlet says when he is alone with the ghost, "I am bound to hear," and the ghost in his reply picks up the significant word "bound" and throws it back at the prince: "So art thou to revenge, when thou shalt hear" (I.v.6–7).

Once again we are dealing with a scene built around a centerpiece. The first segment, running 91 lines, is introductory and is usually printed, improperly, as a separate scene (I.iv). The central segment, running 112 lines, is the interview with the ghost and Hamlet's vow of revenge, the second soliloquy ("O all you host of heaven!"). After this, Horatio and Marcellus reenter for a concluding segment which balances the first, running 78 lines. In the center of the fourth scene, then, as in the center of the third, is a father giving advice to a son. And, lest we miss the ironic link between the two scenes, Shakespeare provides a verbal echo, Hamlet's vow to wipe everything but his father's commandment from the table of his memory, the book and volume of his brain, recalling Polonius' insistence on memory and in fact developing the same metaphor of inscription: "And these few precepts in thy memory / Look thou character" (I.iii.58–59).

The structure of the fourth scene echoes the first and second as well. The central panel is the vivid picture that the ghost paints of himself sleeping in his orchard while Claudius creeps in to pour the "leperous distilment" in his ears, a picture foreshadowed by the prophetic images of falling-off in the centerpieces of the first and second scenes. Proceeding from one centerpiece to the next—from Horatio's elegiac image of King Hamlet and King Fortinbras, to Hamlet's contrasting images of Hyperion and the satyr, to the ghost's picture of his poisoning—is not entirely unlike proceeding past two typological Old Testament panels and at last arriving at the New Testament scene they foreshadow. "O my prophetic soul!" Hamlet exclaims as the ghost's revelations fulfill the ominous premonitions we have felt from the play's beginning. Moreover, now the "sullied flesh" theme, the frequent hints of physical decay, of something rotten in Denmark, is also fulfilled as the ghost describes how "a most instant tetter barked about / Most lazar-like with vile and loathsome crust / All my smooth body" (I.v.71–73). Claudius' poison has transformed King Hamlet, image of the ideal, into a figure of horror and agony. Perhaps we should not worry ourselves overmuch about whether Shakespeare's audience believed in Purgatory, or, for that matter, ghosts. Nor need we speculate about what "foul crimes" King Hamlet might have committed while alive. In the central panel of this scene, the ghost's portrait of himself, doomed to walk the night and confined to fast in fire by day, is another image of the total corruption of nobility resulting from Claudius' original sin. Like the prince, and like Denmark itself in the usurper's grasp, King Hamlet, locked in his mysterious "prison house," has lost his freedom.

In the final segment offstage sounds again figure prominently, the ghost's cries from the cellarage balancing the sound of the king's cannon earlier. Hamlet can no more escape his father's spirit than he can his uncle's. The scene as a whole thus resolves itself into a picture similar in some respects to that of the second scene, where the prince is trapped between Claudius on one side and King Hamlet on the other:

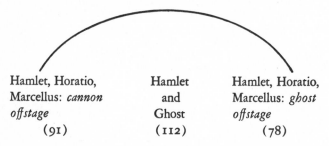

Hamlet, Horatio, Marcellus: *cannon offstage*	Hamlet and Ghost	Hamlet, Horatio, Marcellus: *ghost offstage*
(91)	(112)	(78)

The "vicious mole of nature" speech before the ghost's appearance suggested Hamlet's vague premonitions about the curse of his nativity. The scene returns to this subject at its conclusion, but the fears are no longer vague: "The time is out of joint. O cursed spite / That ever I was born to set it right!" (I.v.188–189).

This couplet, summing up the action so far, puts a period to the play's first phase. Each of the first four scenes is designed on the frame principle, and each can be examined as an independently organized "picture." But the four scenes are closely connected in theme, all gravitating, as we have seen, toward the same concerns: freedom, danger, and the great falling-off that has transformed the world of the play. This shared center of gravity is one reason for the coherence of the group. Another is the superimposed pattern of alternation between episodes concerned with the mystery of the ghost and those concerned with the apparently normal world of the Danish court.

5. Polonius: "Finding Out" (II.i)

The fifth scene introduces the "finding out" theme of the second phase, which is principally concerned with the intellectual duel between Hamlet and Claudius, the attempt of each to play upon the other, to pluck out the heart of the other's mystery. The scene begins with Polonius' conversation with Reynaldo, whom he is sending to spy on Laertes. Just as Hamlet cannot escape his father's spirit, so Laertes cannot escape Polonius. The design of the scene keeps the pairing of the two sons before us, the first segment showing Polonius concerned about Laertes and the second, in which Ophelia reports Hamlet's appearance in her closet, showing him concerned about the prince.

Polonius reckons himself a master at devious intrigue, but even as he is pompously explaining to Reynaldo how to use indirections to find directions out, Shakespeare deflates him with a lapse in memory: "What was I about to say? By the mass, I was about to say something!" (50–51). The last time we saw Polonius he was charging Laertes to remember his precepts, and his memory lapse here is perhaps a comment on his hasty conclusion that Hamlet is mad for Ophelia's love.

6. *Claudius versus Hamlet (II.ii)*

Polonius is a foil for the more subtle intriguers, Claudius and Hamlet. The spy motif forms the liaison between the fifth scene and the sixth, which opens with Claudius interviewing Rosencrantz and Guildenstern, suggesting that they draw Hamlet "on to pleasures" in order to discover by indirection the nature of his affliction. Claudius' tactics are the same as Polonius', but his manner is entirely different. It is his discipline, his self-control, that makes him dangerous.

The sixth scene, running nearly 600 lines, is the longest in the play. As Alfred Harbage points out, it is unified by theme, beginning with Claudius, his mind focused on Hamlet, and ending with the prince, his mind focused on Claudius.[3] The symmetrical organization encourages us to compare Claudius and Hamlet, for if Claudius is subtle and dangerous, Hamlet is even more so. The scene falls into three long segments: in the first, running 169 lines, Claudius prepares his instruments, Rosencrantz, Guildenstern, and Polonius; in the middle, running 241 lines, Hamlet parries Claudius' indirect thrusts, meeting and defeating each of the spies; and in the final segment, running 181 lines, he prepares his own instruments, the actors.

The Claudius segment begins with the Rosencrantz and Guildenstern interview and ends with Polonius' proposal to "loose" Ophelia to test Hamlet. Between these two episodes Claudius receives the ambassadors, who report their success in diverting young Fortinbras' attentions to the Polack. At first the ambassadors may seem an extraneous element, but in fact, as legitimate go-betweens, they are foils for Claudius' other "ambassadors." Moreover, their success in Norway contrasts significantly with Rosencrantz, Guildenstern, and Polonius' utter failure with Hamlet in the middle of the scene.

The long middle section begins with Hamlet's entrance, at which point Polonius hustles Claudius and Gertrude offstage so that he can "board" the prince alone. In the "fishmonger scene," as this episode is often called, Hamlet runs rings around the ingenuous old man, mocking his stupidity. This Hamlet-Polonius episode is balanced by another at the end of the middle section when Polonius reenters to announce the actors' arrival. The two Polonius sections frame the central conversation with Rosencrantz and Guildenstern:

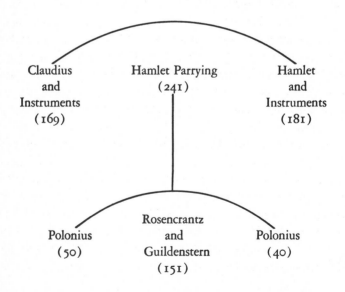

Claudius and Instruments (169)

Hamlet Parrying (241)

Hamlet and Instruments (181)

Polonius (50)

Rosencrantz and Guildenstern (151)

Polonius (40)

With Polonius, whose inability to dissimulate or conceal his thoughts makes him a perfect foil, Hamlet plays the lunatic. With Rosencrantz and Guildenstern, however, he tries to be frank until he realizes that his old friends are also the king's tools, that they are acting roles, and then with a direct thrust—"Were you not sent for?" (271)—the prince pierces their disguise.

The sixth scene is organized so that the initiative passes from Claudius to Hamlet in the middle. Simultaneously, there is a shift in the scene's dominant motif from go-betweens and spies to Hamlet's characteristic weaponry—actors and acting. The acting motif, implicit in the Hamlet-Polonius colloquy, becomes explicit about midway in the Rosencrantz-Guildenstern interview when Rosencrantz reveals that the players are coming to offer Hamlet "service." This leads to the discussion of the boy actors tyrannizing over the stage, a subject perhaps introduced principally for its contemporary interest but related in theme to the general concern with decay.

The arrival of the professional players brings home to Hamlet the nature of the role in which he has been cast by birth. Much of the scene's final segment is taken up by the "player's speech," the description of Pyrrhus' bloody vengeance for his father's death. The prince evidently requests this speech because he sees in the crash of father Priam an image of his own father's fall, and, in the grief of Hecuba, the "mobled queen," an image of how Queen Gertrude ought to have behaved after her husband's death. More interesting, in Pyrrhus he sees a reflection of his own role, and significantly it is Hamlet himself who enacts the first dozen lines describing the dismal heraldry of the revenger.

The final segment concludes with a coda, the third soliloquy ("O, what a rogue and peasant slave am I!"), in which Hamlet examines his performance so far in explicitly theatrical terms. The prince has not, by and large, indulged in much cleaving of the general ear with horrid speech in the conventional manner of a revenger, and his aristocratic contempt for such a manner is implicit in his description of what the common player would do with his motive and cue for passion, amazing the very faculties of eyes and ears and drowning the stage with tears. Fully aware of the need for caution and restraint with an opponent like Claudius, Hamlet has been playing the part in his own style. Yet he wonders now if his judicious silence means simply that he is unpregnant of his cause, and, as if to prove to himself that this is not so, winds himself up to a bout of ranting rhetoric, challenging some invisible observer to call him coward, pluck his beard, tweak his nose, and finally hurling at Claudius a passionate stream of epithets: "Bloody, bawdy villain! / Remorseless, treacherous, lecherous, kindless villain! / O, vengeance!" (565–567). Here the prince breaks off, cursing himself for a whore, a drab. Rant accomplishes nothing: what is presently required is not the player's whorish art but action. Moreover, he must be certain that his own situation is not just a fiction, a dream of passion, that the spirit he has seen is truly his father. And so, with superb irony in his choice of means, Hamlet reveals what his form of action is to be: "I'll have these players / Play something like the murder of my father / Before mine uncle" (580–582).

7. Hamlet Observed (III.i)

The sixth scene concludes with Hamlet proposing to observe the king at the play; the seventh, in which Claudius and Polonius put the arras-plot into practice, shows us the king observing Hamlet. It is in this scene, while the king and Polonius are peering from behind the curtain, that Ophelia, with unconscious irony, refers to Hamlet as the "observed of all observers" (154).

The scene opens with Claudius hearing Rosencrantz and Guildenstern report their failure with Hamlet, and closes with Claudius again in the foreground, having succeeded only slightly better himself: "Love? his affections do not that way tend" (162). Framed by the corrupt court characters, Hamlet in the long central panel expresses his revulsion and despair in the "To be, or not to be" soliloquy and the "Get thee to a nunnery" conversation with Ophelia. "T'have seen what I have seen, see what I see!" (161) Ophelia exclaims in pity for Hamlet, but the point is that she does not see at all. The scene is designed to suggest the distance between Hamlet's complex sensibility and the more limited minds of his observers, to whom he is more or less opaque, even when caught off guard. The precise psychological function of the "To be, or not to be" soliloquy—that is, why Hamlet is considering suicide —is uncertain. But its dramatic function is not: the speech, however we interpret it, is conspicuously "deep," and it establishes the prince as more thoughtful than those around him.

8. *Claudius Observed: The Mousetrap (III.ii)*

In the eighth scene Hamlet succeeds where Claudius has failed: he exposes the heart of his enemy's mystery. The mousetrap, running nearly 400 lines, is one of the longest and most carefully designed scenes in the play. It begins with Hamlet's address to the players, which establishes its dominant motif, playing, and its dominant theme—discipline, self-control. Hamlet's taste, as we know from his conversation with the actors, is for plays like that from which the Pyrrhus speech comes, plays written with as much "modesty"—by which he means restraint—as cunning. His taste in acting is similarly refined. Lines are to be spoken "trippingly on the tongue"—that is, with grace—rather than clumsily "mouthed" in the fashion of a town crier. Nor should the player permit himself gross gestures, like sawing the air with his hand; rather he must "use all gently," and even in the very torrent, tempest, and whirlwind of passion—the moment of extremity when the temptation to strut and bellow is greatest—must "acquire and beget a temperance that may give it smoothness" (7–8). The actor who tears a passion to tatters may win the applause of the groundlings, who are only amused by noise, but he is worse than Termagant or Herod, those proverbially noisy characters of the old mystery plays, which Hamlet disdains as ignorant and vulgar drama. "Discretion" is the key to excellent acting.

The advice to the players is Hamlet's version of Polonius' advice to Laertes to be discreet. The speech permits him to comment indirectly on his most vital concern, how one ought to play the part of a revenger. Hamlet's difficulty is aesthetic. His problem is one of form and content, of suiting the action to the word, the word to the action, that is, of finding a satisfactory shape for his revenge. To strut and bellow in order to prove his passion would be not only aesthetically offensive but dangerous, because he is locked in a mortal struggle in which self-control means everything. There is a further issue as well. Hamlet is committed to all that the play's opening image of the two valiant kings face to face in royal combat implies—the conception of man noble in reason, godlike in action and apprehension. Undisciplined acting is not merely poor art, but an offense against the "modesty of nature." "O, there be players that I have seen play ... that neither having th'accent of Christians, nor the gait of Christian, pagan, nor man, have so strutted and bellowed that I have thought some of Nature's journeymen had made men, and not made them well, they imitated humanity so abominably" (23–33). To rage and rant is to make oneself into a monster. Hamlet cannot escape the role of revenger, but he can at least play it in a style that does not offend his conception of human dignity.

The themes of the address to the players are restated in the conversation with Horatio, which immediately follows. The address is largely negative, a picture of what Hamlet disdains. The praise of Horatio, the "just" man, gives us Hamlet's ideal of neo-Stoic self-control. In the terms of this segment, human dignity is seen as a matter of freedom. One cannot be passionless, but one can refuse to become passion's slave. One cannot avoid fortune, but one can refuse to be a "pipe for Fortune's finger / To sound what stop she please" (67–68).

The two opening episodes, the address to the players and the praise of Horatio, form a prologue which prepares us for the scene's central panel, the mousetrap itself, in which Hamlet demonstrates that he can play upon Claudius like a pipe and make him bellow. The scene is designed so that the opening episodes are balanced by corresponding episodes after the central panel: again we have a conversation between Hamlet and Horatio, followed by the episode usually called the "recorder scene," in which the pipe image of the opening section is made concrete. Possibly Hamlet's request for the recorders is an attempt to reenact his triumph symbolically. In any case, Rosencrantz and Guildenstern enter and once again fail in their mission:

Why, look you now, how unworthy a thing you make of me! You would play upon me, you would seem to know my stops, you would pluck out the heart of my mystery, you would sound me from my lowest note to the top of my compass; and there is much music, excellent voice, in this little organ, yet cannot you make it speak. 'Sblood, do you think I am easier to be played on than a pipe? Call me what instrument you will, though you can fret me, you cannot play upon me. (349–357)

Immediately, Hamlet turns to Polonius, who has just entered, and leads the old courtier through the game of cloud shapes, making him see the cloud first as a camel, then as a weasel, and finally as a whale. Though Claudius and his instruments cannot play upon him, Hamlet is contemptuously demonstrating that he can make any of them sound what tune he pleases.

The scene as a whole thus resolves itself into a picture composed of three major segments, the opening and closing sections framing and helping to explain the central panel:

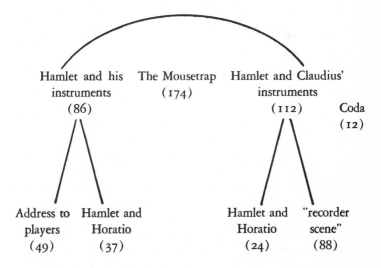

Hamlet and his instruments (86)   The Mousetrap (174)   Hamlet and Claudius' instruments (112)   Coda (12)

Address to players (49)   Hamlet and Horatio (37)   Hamlet and Horatio (24)   "recorder scene" (88)

Structurally, the mousetrap scene echoes both preceding scenes, the sixth and the seventh: in each case the centerpiece shows an important thrust in the duel between the mighty opposites. Twice Hamlet parries; once he thrusts, scoring a palpable hit.

The mousetrap scene, in which Hamlet's fortunes reach their apex, is the turning point of the play. Before it, Hamlet and Claudius circle each other warily, each trying to find out how much the other knows. After it, they are no longer probing but trying to murder each other. The first movement is tentative and questioning, the second more direct and deadly. Soon after the mousetrap the first death occurs as Hamlet accidentally murders Polonius, initiating a new revenge action.

In the pivotal center of the play, Shakespeare gives us a direct statement of theme. The central panel falls into three segments: first the exchange of comments between Hamlet and the other members of the audience as they are settling down for the performance, then the play itself from the dumb show to the player queen's exit, and finally another section in which audience comments dominate until Claudius' cry for lights disperses the assembly.

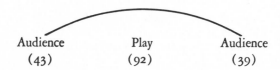

Audience   Play   Audience
(43)   (92)   (39)

In the middle segment, roughly in the center of the scene and the play as a whole, the player king lectures his queen on the inconstancy of human purposes:

> I do believe you think what now you speak,
> But what we do determine oft we break.
> Purpose is but the slave to memory,
> Of violent birth, but poor validity,
> Which now like fruit unripe sticks on the tree,
> But fall unshaken when they mellow be.
> Most necessary 'tis that we forget
> To pay ourselves what to ourselves is debt.
> What to ourselves in passion we propose,

> The passion ending, doth the purpose lose.
> The violence of either grief or joy
> Their own enactures with themselves destroy . . .
> Our wills and fates do so contrary run
> That our devices still are overthrown;
> Our thoughts are ours, their ends none of our own.   (178–205)

Critics have suggested from time to time that the player king's lecture, unnecessary to the plot of *The Murder of Gonzago,* is perhaps the speech of some dozen or sixteen lines composed by Hamlet, but the whole issue of which speech Hamlet may have written is somewhat beside the point. More interesting is to note that this speech, an explicit exposition of some of the play's central ideas, occupies perhaps the most emphatic position in the entire tragedy.

Like the player king, Hamlet distrusts purposes proposed in passion, and much of the internal drama of the first half of the play has stemmed from his war with himself, his struggle to reduce his whirlwind passion to smoothness. The mousetrap scene concludes with a brief coda, the twelve-line soliloquy in which Hamlet once again sounds the conventional revenger's note but then quickly recovers himself:

> 'Tis now the very witching time of night,
> When churchyards yawn, and hell itself breathes out
> Contagion to this world. Now could I drink hot blood
> And do such bitter business as the day
> Would quake to look on. Soft, now to my mother.
> O heart, lose not thy nature; let not ever
> The soul of Nero enter this firm bosom.   (373–379)

Hamlet knows that the king is guilty, but even so he means to maintain proportion in his acts.

9. *The Prayer Scene (III.iii)*

The relatively short ninth scene opens the second movement by showing Claudius and Hamlet each attempting to send the other on a journey, Hamlet to England and Claudius to hell. Neither will accomplish his purpose in the way he intends.

If the first half of the play has emphasized Hamlet's dignity, his insistence upon shaping his revenge and his life according to his own standards, the second emphasizes the degree to which will and fate are contrary. When Laertes in the third scene, saying much more than he realizes, warns Ophelia that Hamlet may not "carve" for himself, Shakespeare perhaps has in mind the imagery of *Julius Caesar* and Brutus' pledge to be a sacrificer rather than a butcher, to carve Caesar as a dish fit for the gods, for, like Hamlet, Brutus is concerned with the manner of his carving. But the word is also Shakespeare's term for sculptor, and perhaps even this early in the play he is trying to suggest that Hamlet is a kind of artist. Yet in the carving of his revenge only Hamlet's thoughts are entirely his own: there is, he discovers, "a divinity that shapes our ends, / Rough-hew them how we will" (V.ii.10–11).

Confronted with the king on his knees, Hamlet exercises restraint, for it seems to him that to dispatch Claudius fit and seasoned for his passage would be folly. Hamlet exits and Claudius rises to reveal that his thoughts are mundane. Shakespeare has used dramatic irony against every major character in the play, but this is the first time he employs it against Hamlet, and the irony, moreover, is not subtle.

10. *The Closet Scene (III.iv-IV.1)*[4]

Having refused to murder the king at a moment so propitious that it must seem providential, Hamlet chooses his own moment to act and kills the wrong man. To punctuate his bungling, the ghost reappears, and it is now that the issue of delay is emphatically raised as Hamlet accuses himself of having let the time slip and his passion wane.

The reappearance of the ghost is important structurally, helping to indicate, as Bradley noted, that the play is making a new beginning.[5] The ghost occupies the emphatic central position in the scene, framed by the segments in which Hamlet berates his mother, and also by the opening segment, in which the chief event is Polonius' death, and the concluding conversation between Claudius and Gertrude:

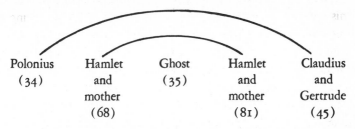

| Polonius (34) | Hamlet and mother (68) | Ghost (35) | Hamlet and mother (81) | Claudius and Gertrude (45) |

The ghost, which probably because of her moral blindness Gertrude cannot see, is also the pivot on which the scene turns: before its appearance the queen is reluctant to listen to her son's accusations; after it, she submits completely, asking merely, "What shall I do?" (III.iv.181). Indeed, the scene as a whole is designed to suggest the queen's change of heart: it opens with her deceiving Hamlet by allowing Polonius to overhear their conversation, but concludes with her deceiving Claudius to protect her son.

Gertrude's anguished question, "What shall I do?" can perhaps be seen as applying to Hamlet as well. The prince, having failed to shape his revenge according to his will, knows only what not to do. Significantly, his reply to Gertrude is couched in negative terms:

> Not this, by no means, that I bid you do:
> Let the bloat king tempt you again to bed,
> Pinch wanton on your cheek, call you his mouse,
> And let him, for a pair of reechy kisses,
> Or paddling in your neck with his damned fingers,
> Make you to ravel all this matter out.   (III.iv.182–187)

Immediately, the conversation turns from Gertrude's to Hamlet's problem as the prince remarks that he is being sent to England. He believes now that he must deliver himself to providence, trusting that, if heaven intends him for its scourge and minister, Claudius' treachery will somehow play into his hands.

11, 12, and 13 (IV.ii-iv)

The flow of action from the final segment of the closet scene to the brief eleventh scene, in which Rosencrantz and Guildenstern pursue Hamlet across the stage, is almost continuous, as is the flow from the eleventh to the twelfth, in which the captured prince is brought before Claudius. A third brief scene follows, in which Fortinbras' appearance gives rise to Hamlet's seventh soliloquy ("How all occasions do inform against me").

Shakespeare often uses a series of rapid, brief scenes to convey an impression of speed. Here Hamlet is being hustled off to England, and the rapid scenes introduce an important note of frenzy. Hamlet's taunting of Rosencrantz and Guildenstern in the eleventh scene and his wild rush across the stage—"Hide fox, and all after" (IV.ii.29–30)—make a mockery of Claudius, his instruments, and his plan. In the interview with Claudius he goes further and makes a mockery of all mortal purposes and illusions of power: "We fat all creatures else to fat us, and we fat ourselves for maggots. Your fat king and your lean beggar is but variable service—two dishes, but to one table. That's the end" (IV.iii.21–25). Hamlet's frenzy is of course to some degree a mask, a return to the antic disposition at a higher pitch, but it is also his way of commenting upon what he now, after the murder of Polonius, sees as the absurdity of human pretensions, his own as well as Claudius'. The thirteenth scene, however, rapidly qualifies the perspective of the eleventh and twelfth even as it continues the same general theme. Fortinbras' army solemnly marching to debate the question of a straw is an emblem of mortal absurdity but at the same time a reminder that man is more than meat for worms, and Hamlet sees in the Norwegian prince a personal rebuke for forgetting that his honor is at the stake.

The seventh soliloquy, Hamlet's last, puts a period to the momentary frenzy of the eleventh and twelfth scenes and marks the conclusion, too, of the phase which began with the prayer scene and Hamlet's failure to kill Claudius. In this phase Hamlet, who seemed almost omnipotent in the mousetrap, has suffered one of the severest natural shocks that flesh is heir to—the discovery that, however godlike he may be in some respects, he is not divine. The soliloquy ends with Hamlet vowing to be firm in his purpose: "O, from this time forth, / My thoughts be bloody, or be nothing worth" (IV.iv.65–66). It is interesting that Hamlet says "thoughts" rather than "deeds": possibly we are to hear an echo of the player king's remark about will and fate, that only our thoughts are finally subject to our own determination. At any rate, Hamlet departs for England with the problem of his task placed in larger perspective.

14. The Polonii Mad (IV.v)

The action in the play's final phase is largely concerned with Laertes' revenge, and if we have any doubts about whether Hamlet would have been more successful if he had been a different kind of revenger, one less given to thinking precisely on the event, they are quieted here. Faced with a situation similar to Hamlet's the relatively simple-minded Polonii break down. Ophelia, unable to control her grief, lapses into madness and a muddy death, reminding us that it is one of Hamlet's achievements that he does not go mad but only plays at insanity to disguise his true strength. And Laertes goes mad in a different fashion, becoming the model of the kind of ranting, passionate revenger that Hamlet disdains.

The fourteenth scene is perhaps designed to echo the third, in which so much complacent advice was passed from hand to hand. Again, two Ophelia episodes frame a central section concerned with Laertes: first Ophelia displays her madness to the king and queen (96 lines); then Laertes bursts in demanding revenge (56 lines); and finally Ophelia returns for another madness episode, the passing out of flowers (65 lines). Naturally, the two Ophelia episodes help to shape our understanding of the Laertes center-piece.

Hamlet knows that he is, in a sense, playing a role as revenger, but Laertes is blissfully unselfconscious of his part. Laertes—to adapt Nashe's famous allusion to Kyd's old *Hamlet*—if you entreat him fair in a frosty morning, will shamelessly afford you handfuls of tragical speeches, ranting in the best manner of English Seneca:

> To hell allegiance, vows to the blackest devil,
> Conscience and grace to the profoundest pit!
> I dare damnation. To this point I stand,
> That both the worlds I give to negligence,
> Let come what comes, only I'll be revenged
> Most throughly for my father. (IV.v.131–136)

What comes is not quite the revenge Laertes expects, for the situation is not so simple as he supposes; rather he finds himself on account of his unthinking passion an easy instrument for Claudius to play, becoming, in his own word, the king's "organ."

15 and 16. Escape and Drowning (IV.vi-vii)

The fourteenth scene is part of a designed group of three scenes in which Hamlet is absent. As many have observed, the fourteenth scene, which concludes with Claudius and Laertes departing for a private conversation, and the sixteenth, in which they stroll onstage in the midst of that conversation, represent a single continuous action. What would normally be one scene is split by the interjection of the brief episode in which Horatio receives Hamlet's letter telling of the pirate ship and his return to Denmark.

The sixteenth scene ends as the fourteenth began, with the focus on Ophelia as Gertrude describes her drowning. Oblivious of her peril, the mad girl quietly yields to the waters that draw her down. Laertes, too, has yielded to Claudius, and the group as a whole thus resolves itself into a large balanced picture in which the "sinking" of the Polonii contrasts with the brief but emphatic central panel describing Hamlet's escape from treacherous waters:

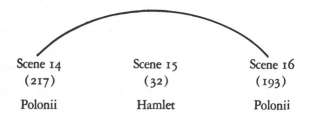

Scene 14	Scene 15	Scene 16
(217)	(32)	(193)
Polonii	Hamlet	Polonii

17. The Graveyard Scene (V.i)

The penultimate scene begins with the comic debate between the gravediggers on the definition of suicide. When is a man responsible for his own death? "Here lies the water—good. Here stands the man—good. If the man go to this water and drown himself, it is, will he nill he, he goes, mark you that. But if the water come to him and drown him, he drowns not himself. Argal, he that is not guilty of his own death shortens not his own life" (13–18). In other words, what is suicide but killing oneself? Reminiscent of Polonius' definition of madness, this simplistic thinking emphasizes by its inadequacy the problematic nature of Ophelia's death: is she or is she not responsible? At the same time, it looks forward to the problematic nature of Hamlet's final act, when the "water" in effect comes to him as he consents to the mortal duel. Is he or is he not responsible for his revenge?

The clowns' dialogue forms a prologue, running 57 lines. The first segment of the scene proper begins with Hamlet's entrance asking whether the singing gravedigger has no feeling for his work. Just as the image of Fortune's pipe becomes concrete in the recorder episode, so the imagery of mortality, of the common end of fat kings and lean beggars, introduced in the twelfth scene becomes concrete here. Now, after the sea voyage, the frenzy is gone, and Hamlet's sense of the absurdity of mortal pretention is tempered with Olympian pity, the recognition that the skull the gravedigger "jowls" heartlessly to the ground "had a tongue in it, and could sing once" (71–72). The emblematic tableau of Hamlet in the graveyard provides an objective realization of the prince's present state of mind, looking "before and after" with a discourse godlike in its largeness.

The prince's equilibrium is abruptly shattered, however, by another of the shocks that flesh is heir to: the corpse for which the grave waits is Ophelia's. From the long perspective of eternity the scene returns to the immediacy of the present, and Hamlet flies into a towering passion as, according to the probably authentic stage direction of the first quarto, he leaps into the grave to proclaim his love for Ophelia. The scene as a whole is thus a diptych, the picture of Hamlet standing quietly with the skull in his hand balanced against the picture of him struggling in the grave with Laertes, a foreshadowing of the play's end.

Hamlet's struggle with Laertes is a reversion to his earlier and fiercer mood, the proud, contemptuous spirit of the mousetrap scene. Simultaneously, Shakespeare, contrasting his two revengers, the commonplace Laertes and the extraordinary Hamlet, delicately recalls the theatrical motif that dominated the middle part of the play. The prince finds Laertes, true to form, tearing a passion to tatters, bellowing to be buried alive with his sister. Hamlet steps forward and the technical rhetorical terms he uses, "emphasis" and "phrase," together with the simile of making the stars stand like "wonder-wounded hearers," like an audience, reveal his critical attitude, his professional interest in the quality of Laertes' performance:

> What he is whose grief
> Bears such an emphasis? whose phrase of sorrow
> Conjures the wand'ring stars, and makes them stand
> Like wonder-wounded hearers? This is I,
> Hamlet the Dane.   (241–245)

Suiting outrageous word to outrageous action, Hamlet challenges Laertes to a contest of noise, of rant. What will Laertes do to prove his love for Ophelia, weep, tear himself, drink vinegar, eat a crocodile? Hamlet will match him. Does Laertes mean to whine, to prate of being buried under a mountain higher than Pelion? Why, then Hamlet will say he'll be buried too, and let the imaginary mountain be so high that it touches the sphere of fire and makes Ossa by comparison a wart. "Nay, an thou'lt mouth," the prince says, using the same word with which he had earlier described the manner of vulgar actors, "I'll rant as well as thou" (270–271). Hamlet is mocking Laertes' style, but the bitterness of his mockery, the nastiness of it, derives from his sincere grief for Ophelia.

18. The Finale (V.ii)

The rhythm of the graveyard scene is repeated in the finale. Again a relatively detached and contemplative segment in which Hamlet and Horatio are together precedes a more active segment in which Hamlet is pitted against Laertes. The theme of the finale is stated immediately as Hamlet, describing his providential escape from Rosencrantz and Guildenstern, comments on the divinity that shapes our ends.

This conversation reestablishes Hamlet's calm and large perspective. Before he is put to the final test, however, the duel with Laertes, Shakespeare introduces that impossible fop, Osric, the emblem of the empty courtesy of Claudius' court. Just as Hamlet earlier led Polonius through the game of cloud shapes, so now he toys with Osric, leading him to proclaim first that the weather is warm, then that it is cold, and finally warm again. The prince is demonstrating that if he wished he might still play upon the king and his instruments like so many pipes. Nevertheless, Hamlet's mood is changed from the preceding scene: rather than outrage, he feels only amused contempt for Osric's pretentious manner. Osric is the quintessential man of the moment, the singer of every current tune, and Hamlet, as he himself seems to realize, is on the verge of eternity. Why should he bother himself about a waterfly spacious in the possession of dirt? The prince accepts the king's invitation calmly, no longer insisting that he alone must shape his life, and the first half of the scene ends on the same calm note with which it began: "If it be now, 'tis not to come; if it be not to come, it will be now; if it be not now, yet it will come. The readiness is all. Since no man of aught he leaves knows, what is't to leave betimes? Let be" (209–213).

The quiet first segment composed of the conversation with Horatio and the Osric episode, together running 213 lines, is sharply distinguished from the final court segment, roughly equivalent in length, against which it is balanced. Significantly, the king and court enter to Hamlet, his fate seeking him out rather than the other way round; the prince merely stands waiting while the elaborate properties for the duel are prepared.

Theatrical imagery is again prominent in this segment, for the duel is Claudius' poisoned play as the mousetrap was Hamlet's, and possibly the staging should recall the earlier scene, with Hamlet and Laertes playing in the same part of the stage as the actors earlier. The ominous sound of Claudius' cannon speaking to the heavens as Hamlet scores the first hit also recalls earlier parts of the tragedy. Most important, however, the duel recalls the prologue and the image of King Hamlet and King Fortinbras contending for their countries' honor and fortune. King Hamlet fought his single combat in an unfallen world of law and heraldry; his son must seek to emulate him in a world of empty chivalry and poisoned foils; and yet, in its way, Hamlet's duel with Laertes is as heroic as his father's with Fortinbras, and in his own manner the prince proves himself worthy of the name "Hamlet" and a soldier's honors. Constant to his purpose until the end, Hamlet at last accomplishes his revenge, but the conclusion of this second combat is the destruction of all the principals of Denmark, Hamlet and Laertes as well as Claudius and Gertrude, through the poison with which Claudius has infected the state. Hamlet is the victor, as his father was before him, but, ironically, this time it is Fortinbras who gathers the spoils.

The "full circle" technique, the expanded epanalepsis in which the end harks back to the beginning, has much the same effect on the level of the play as it has on individual scenes. It produces a sense of completeness, of having followed to the end an entire cycle in human affairs, and it brings back the two or three hours of traffic of the stage for contemplation as a whole.

Hamlet is one of Shakespeare's most reflexive, most theatrically self-conscious plays. So pervasive is the concern with theater that, as many since Maynard Mack have noted, simple terms like "show," "act," "play," and "perform" seem drawn toward their specifically theatrical meanings even when they occur in neutral contexts. Nearly every character from the ghost to the king is at some time or another seen metaphorically as an actor maintaining a façade to hide a deeper reality within, and this repeated motif contributes significantly to the impression of layer within layer of reality, boxes within boxes, that the play projects. It is perhaps helpful, then, to observe that *Hamlet* is literally built around the all-the-world's-a-stage metaphor, concretely realized in the mousetrap, which divides the play into two roughly equal movements.

Initial movement (1748)	Mousetrap scene (384)	Latter movement (1644)

Three major scenes define the overall design—the opening (I.ii), the mousetrap, and the finale. Each is a long and elaborately patterned scene in which Hamlet and Claudius confront each other as deadly enemies before an uncomprehending world. Furthermore, each is a formal court scene in which the stage is full. Symmetrically disposed at the beginning, middle, and end, these three scenes stand out as, structurally, the most important panels in a composition made of many parts. And in the heart of the composition is the heart of the mystery, a central emblem for which the entire tragedy is the frame—the tableau of the court watching *The Murder of Gonzago,* the mirror of their lives, even as we are watching *Hamlet,* the mirror of our own.

5

The Early Plays

The overall shapeliness of *Hamlet*—and of the plays I discussed in the first chapter, *A Midsummer Night's Dream* and *The Winter's Tale*—is characteristic of Shakespeare's work. The three plays represent different genres and periods—a romantic comedy from the middle 1590's, a turn-of-the-century tragedy, and a late romance. But in each case the key to the design is what we can call Shakespeare's "feeling for the center"—the forest sequence in *A Midsummer Night's Dream;* the long, pivotal, mousetrap scene in *Hamlet;* the great gap of time in *The Winter's Tale.*

The *Hamlet* pattern is the most common in Shakespeare. Most often we will find, in approximately the center of the play, a long, elaborately designed scene, such as the tavern scene in *1 Henry IV,* Bassanio's casket choice in *The Merchant of Venice,*[1] or the temptation scene in *Othello,* around which the play as a whole is shaped. It seems plausible to suppose that one of Shakespeare's first problems in organizing his material was to decide, at least tentatively, what this central scene was to be. Very frequently, as in *Hamlet,* there will be emphatic links, structural or thematic echoes, between the opening, central scene, and finale. In *Romeo and Juliet,* for instance, these three scenes are the only ones in which the prince appears. In *Lear* the opening and finale are the only scenes in which the royal family are together. The opening, central scene, and finale, when all three are emphatic, form the pillars on which the architecture of the whole rests.

Early History Plays

The sure sense of design that Shakespeare reveals in *Hamlet* is the product of experience and experiment. From the start of his career Shakespeare possessed a feeling for the scene as a unit and was able to organize even fairly long dramatic segments, such as the Battle of Towton sequence, into expressive patterns. The earliest plays do not, however, always show him in firm control of overall design. Assuming, as most recent scholars do, that Shakespeare is the sole author of the *Henry VI* trilogy, and that these plays and *Richard III* were written in chronological order, it is possible to observe play by play some of his earliest experiments with design.

1 Henry VI is above all a play of individual scenes. Each scene is a lucidly organized composition related to the play's controlling theme, the spread of dissension and the decay of English power. The first scene, for example, opens with the funeral of Henry V, which provides both an arresting spectacle and a concrete symbol of decline, after which Shakespeare brings on a series of messengers bearing progressively worse news from France—the loss of the French towns, the crowning of the dauphin, and finally the capture of the great English general, Talbot. The latter segment is the confirmation of the purport of the opening spectacle, and the scene as a whole effectively introduces the controlling theme. The second scene is a new speaking picture, an ironic portrait of the conquering French. The two scenes are linked by motif, the first beginning with astrological allusions to comets and "bad revolting stars," and the second opening in the same vein:

> Mars his true moving, even as in the heavens
> So in the earth, to this day is not known.
> Late did he shine upon the English side;
> Now we are victors, upon us he smiles.   (I.ii.1–4)

Like the first, this scene consists of two segments. The dauphin attempts to break the siege of Orleans and is roundly defeated by English bravery, after which Joan of Arc is introduced and shown winning command of the French army by overcoming the dauphin in single combat. The scene thus shows two defeats for the dauphin. The point is that it is only because of the dauphin's weakness that the witch has any role in the war at all. The second scene thus qualifies the bleak image of the first, reassuring us that in the field the English are still brave as lions and the French basically incompetent. But, paradoxically, their very weakness gives the French a powerful, and unfair, weapon—the witch.

The third scene is another independent composition in two parts, linked to scene 2 by the siege motif. This scene gives us a picture of the English at home, where the good Duke Humphrey is seeking admission to the Tower, which is controlled by the corrupt Bishop of Winchester. In the first segment the duke and his men rush the Tower gates, attempting unsuccessfully to force entry. In the second the duke and the bishop have a morality-like contention and their men several times skirmish until they are separated by the mayor. The scene thus shows Duke Humphrey twice frustrated in his attempt to work for England's welfare. Scene 2 gave us a siege in France; scene 3 an analogous siege at home. Shakespeare is suggesting that the internal divisions among the English will ultimately cancel out even the remarkable bravery of their soldiers abroad.

1 Henry VI continues in the manner of these three scenes, with each composition internally coherent and giving us a relevant image. The play does not approach a mature work like *1 Henry IV* in subtlety and richness, but it is not wholly different in this aspect of its technique. As Andrew Cairncross puts it, "everything in the play bears witness to careful planning and controlled design."[2]

So it does—but not overall "design" like that of *A Midsummer Night's Dream, 1 Henry IV,* or *Hamlet.* We get a general sense of dissension spreading as the chronicle progresses, but no feeling of a major turning point like the tavern scene or the mousetrap. Instead of a few crucial scenes receiving special emphasis, nearly all appear to receive about the same weight, and this is reflected in the fact that almost all are about the same length. (Of the twenty scenes, eight are between 150 and approximately 200 lines, and none is significantly longer than 200. Nine scenes are between 80 and 150 lines.) The result is that the play as a whole lacks articulation. Shakespeare's feeling for overall symmetry does reveal itself in the repeated motifs which punctuate the beginning, middle, and end. For example, Henry V is dead at the beginning, Mortimer dies near the middle and Talbot toward the end. There is also the "Samson motif" of a man overcome by a woman: at the beginning we see the dauphin defeated by Joan and at the end Henry conquered by Margaret, these episodes contrasting with the scene that comes toward the middle in which Talbot outwits the French countess. But these patterns are not realized in the dramatic structure. Certainly they receive nothing like the kind of emphasis Shakespeare gives to the three "pillars" of *Hamlet*.[3]

The second part of *Henry VI*, which continues the chronicle, dealing with England's internal collapse, is probably Shakespeare's first play with an emphatically marked center. Firm structure naturally depends upon the playwright's having a clear conception of his material, and one reason Shakespeare is able to articulate the overall structure of *2 Henry VI* so well is that in this case not merely particular scenes but the entire story lends itself to a morality-like treatment. Duke Humphrey, the protector of the realm, who dominates the initial movement, personifies justice. His death comes in the play's center, after which Cade and York, representing the destructive forces that law normally restrains, emerge as the dominant figures of the latter movement.

Interestingly, nearly every scene in the play's first half is highly organized, whereas those in the latter movement reveal little internal structure. Typical of the earlier scenes is the fifth (II.i), which contrasts Duke Humphrey's disinterest with the petty malice of the court. Scene 5 is a symmetrical frame scene. The outer panels show Humphrey on the defensive, baited and taunted by Queen Margaret, Cardinal Beaufort, and the Duke of Suffolk. The centerpiece, approximately the same length as the framing segments put together, shows his Solomon-like wisdom as he exposes the fraudulent miracle of the blind man who claims to have had his sight restored by St. Alban.

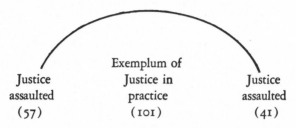

Justice assaulted	Exemplum of Justice in practice	Justice assaulted
(57)	(101)	(41)

Like Othello, circumscribed by Iago, Duke Humphrey is literally surrounded by the enemies of justice. Scenes in the latter movement do not show this kind of design, but are merely episodic, and it seems at least possible that Shakespeare intends this change in technique to be expressive, a reflection of the chaos loosed upon England in the form of Cade and York.

The key to the overall design is the massive centerpiece, which runs nearly 800 lines. This consists of two major scenes, III.i and III.ii, each by itself longer than any other in the play.

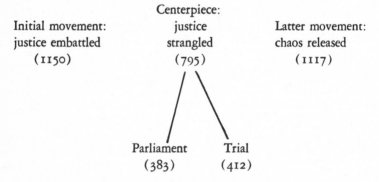

Initial movement: justice embattled	Centerpiece: justice strangled	Latter movement: chaos released
(1150)	(795)	(1117)

Parliament	Trial
(383)	(412)

Both scenes involve formal, legal occasions: II.i is the parliament at which Humphrey is arraigned by his enemies; II.ii is his trial. But the trial is never completed, for between the two scenes the duke is strangled offstage by his enemies. At the arraignment King Henry assures Humphrey that he believes he is innocent, but the duke replies that innocence will not save his life:

Ah, gracious lord, these days are dangerous.
Virtue is choked with foul ambition
And charity chased hence by rancor's hand;
Foul subornation is predominant
And equity exiled your highness' land. (III.i.142–146)

Humphrey's words are prophetic. In the center of the trial scene his corpse is thrust forth onstage, an emblem of how ambition has literally choked virtue. Taken together, the two scenes provide a great "allegorical core"—to adapt the term C. S. Lewis used in connection with Spenser—for the play as a whole.[4]

Possibly this massive centerpiece was also conceived as an allegorical core for the entire *Henry VI* trilogy. In any case it does seem to be the turning point between national decline and open domestic disorder—civil war. At his arraignment, Duke Humphrey himself points out the murder's relationship to the remainder of the trilogy, remarking that his death will be the "prologue" to his enemies' play: "For thousands more, that yet suspect no peril, / Will not conclude their plotted tragedy" (III.i.152–153). Shakespeare evidently has in mind here not only the fighting of the second movement of *2 Henry VI* but the whole of *3 Henry VI* as well. Significantly, the final segment of the parliament scene is the long soliloquy in which York reveals his plan to sieze the crown:

Now, York, or never, steel thy fearful thoughts
And change misdoubt to resolution.
Be that thou hop'st to be; or what thou art
Resign to death: it is not worth th'enjoying. (III.i.331–334)

Placed in the center of *2 Henry VI,* this speech begins the active insurrectionary phase of the chronicle, which is continued in part 3.

The subject of *3 Henry VI* is civil war, the changing tides of fortune as Lancastrians and Yorkists vie for the crown. In this play, too, Shakespeare imposes an overall symmetrical pattern on his material; however, in structure the third part is less successful than the second. The play begins with the Yorkists seizing the throne and compelling King Henry to recognize the Duke of York as his heir. This leads to a counter-action, Queen Margaret's successful Lancastrian offensive in which York is mocked with a paper crown and killed. York's sons retaliate and in the Battle of Towton drive the Lancastrians from the field. The initial movement concludes with King Henry's capture (III.i). The narrative pattern of the first half—Yorkist victory, Lancastrian counter-action, Yorkist retaliation and triumph—is repeated point for point in the second. This begins with III.ii, the scene in which Edward, York's eldest son, first appears as king. Structurally, this scene corresponds to the opening, in which the Duke of York seated himself on Henry's throne. Next comes the counter-action: Queen Margaret consolidates her powers in France, crosses the Channel, and temporarily recovers the throne for Henry. The Yorkists retaliate and in the Battle of Tewkesbury triumph. The action concludes with King Henry's murder in the Tower (V.vi), which corresponds in length and position to the earlier scene in which he was captured. Shakespeare ends the play with a brief coda, the ceremonial scene in which King Edward and Queen Elizabeth take formal possession of the throne (V.vii).

Initial movement: I.i.–III.i			Latter movement: III.ii–V.ii		
(1385)			(1517)		
York seizes throne	Margaret kills York	Battle of Towton	Edward on throne	Margaret recaptures throne	Battle of Tewkesbury

Given the sprawling narrative material, the pattern into which Shakespeare managed to shape his story represents a considerable accomplishment. Nevertheless, there are so many characters and so many separate turning points that the design is hard to see—and, when it is not seen, the play seems chaotic.[5]

The apparent harmony as Edward and his queen celebrate their triumph at the end of *3 Henry VI* is ironic. The hunchback Duke of Gloucester is already hard at work and Shakespeare is looking forward to the next chapter in the chronicle, *Richard III,* which is organized in a somewhat different manner from the *Henry VI* trilogy. This time, after the fashion of Marlowe, Shakespeare focuses on a single dominant character, a procedure that allows him to be more episodic in structure without seeming disorganized. Shakespeare uses this freedom to experiment with shifting the position of the center, delaying the turning point until about two-thirds through the play.

Richard III is built on a rise and fall pattern, the wheel of fortune turning to produce the villain-protagonist's inevitable fall just as it produced his rise. We are introduced to the wheel of fortune in the first scene when Richard, after his opening soliloquy, meets Clarence entering prison and Hastings leaving prison—as Clarence declines, Hastings rises. Throughout the play we trust that Richard, too, must eventually fall. Moreover, we know that there is a providential pattern at work and that his fall will be balanced not by another Richard but by Richmond. Yet the first movement goes on for so long as Richard moves from success to success, rising ever higher on fortune's wheel, that we begin to doubt that he ever will fall. The delayed center generates suspense and irony. The play's structure is designed to create in the audience precisely those fears evoked in *3 Henry VI*—that history is meaningless, an endless parade of cruelty and blood—which the providential ending of the chronicle is intended to allay.

The turning point comes in the seventeenth scene (IV.ii), which for a Shakespearean pivotal scene is remarkably short, running only a little over 100 lines. It is heavily patterned, however, and this lends it weight. Moreover, it is the first time Richard appears as king, and the dramatic effect of the crown and throne should not be underestimated. In *3 Henry VI,* we recall, the midway point was similarly marked by Edward's first appearance with the crown.

The pivotal scene begins with Richard ascending the throne on Buckingham's arm, an action that recapitulates the first movement. Richard and Buckingham, king and king-maker, are at the zenith of their fortunes:

>   Thus high, by thy advice
> And thy assistance, is King Richard seated:
> But shall we wear these glories for a day?
> Or shall they last, and we rejoice in them?   (IV.ii.3–6)

To guarantee his throne Richard commands Buckingham to murder the princes, but the duke hesitates, requesting a moment to consider. Buckingham reenters after 55 lines, having decided to undertake the murder if Richard will grant him the Hereford earldom. But Richard is no longer in the giving vein and the scene ends with the duke, but a few moments earlier the most powerful peer in the realm, in disgrace. In the middle of the scene, while Buckingham is offstage, Richard engages Tyrrel to perform the murder. However, while Tyrrel is being sent for—that is, in the emphatic central position—Richard learns that Richmond's power is growing. When Buckingham returns Richard is preoccupied with premonitions of his own fall: "I do remember me Henry the Sixth / Did prophesy that Richmond should be king" (94–95). The scene as a whole thus resolves itself into an emblematic design, a picture of fortune's turning wheel:

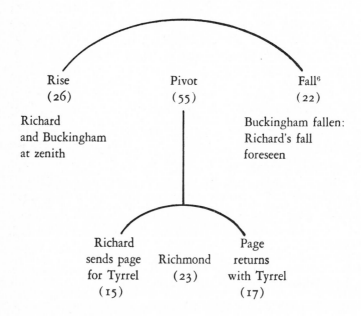

Even as Richard presumes to be a kind of god, to be fortune herself, revolving the wheels of his underlings, his own wheel is turning and his is not the hand in control.

The first history plays show Shakespeare's constructive powers at an early stage in which he seems to be experimenting, not always with complete success, with different methods of overall organization. He never repeated, for example, the delayed center pattern of *Richard III*. *Titus Andronicus* and *Love's Labor's Lost* represent a distinct advance both in the design of individual scenes and in overall organization, and these can perhaps be considered, to employ a word generally used in a rather different sense, Shakespeare's first "regular" plays.

Titus Andronicus and *Love's Labor's Lost*

Titus Andronicus, which T. S. Eliot called "one of the stupidest and most uninspired plays ever written," has long been an embarrassment to Shakespeareans. We can perhaps understand why such a bloody revenge tragedy, stuffed with bombast, was popular in the 1590's. But how is it possible that so crude a play could have been written, as external evidence suggests it was, after *Richard III* and only shortly before the superb "lyrical plays," *A Midsummer Night's Dream, Richard II,* and *Romeo and Juliet?*

Whatever may be said about the verse, characterization, or level of poetic thought, in design *Titus Andronicus* is not crude. On the contrary, it is more clearly articulated than any of the early history plays, with the possible exception of *2 Henry VI,* and in some respects it is a virtuoso performance. The opening scene, for example, is a tour de force. Running over 630 lines, it is the longest scene Shakespeare has yet attempted, and in it he gives us a triumphal procession, a funeral, a human sacrifice, a murder, the election of a Roman emperor, and a great general's fall from power. Dramatic effect is piled on dramatic effect with extraordinary profligacy, yet the artist's shaping hand is firmly in control. Nothing quite like this scene had been written for the Elizabethan stage before.

Great general though he is, Titus' vision, like Lear's or Othello's, is limited, and this results in his destruction. Blind to the differences in character between the late emperor's sons, Saturninus and Bassianus, Titus elects Saturninus emperor on the

basis of external fact alone—Saturninus is the elder. Deaf to Tamora's pleas for mercy, he sacrifices her eldest son in recompense
for his own sons' death. Unjustly, he presents his daughter,
Lavinia, to Saturninus when she is already betrothed to Bassianus.
In the opening scene Titus displays his obtuseness and Shakespeare shows its results.

The scene proper consists of two large panels. In the first Titus
is at the height of his fortune as Rome's hero, the conqueror of
the Goths; in the second he is in decline.

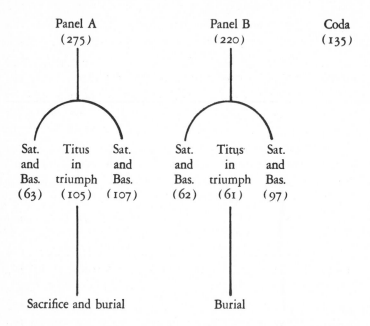

The first panel begins with an elaborately patterned prologue,
the contention between Saturninus and Bassianus discussed earlier
in connection with rhetorical patterning. We can note now that
one effect of the symmetrical prologue is to produce a kind of
double vision. Meticulously paired, the brothers seem identical except in age. But the precise balance encourages us also to take a
closer view in which they appear very different indeed. The long
view is Titus' own perspective, and, having shared it, we can more

readily understand the failure of vision in which he chooses Saturninus. After the prologue, Titus enters in triumph, leading Tamora captive and bringing home the coffin containing his dead sons. Two major actions occur in the centerpiece of this panel: Titus sacrifices Tamora's son and sees his own sons entombed. In the final segment, the play's attention returns to the contending brothers as, asked to choose between them, Titus elects Saturninus and then compounds his mistake by offering him Lavinia's hand. The panel ends with the new emperor's ceremonious exit, accompanied by Tamora and evidently also by the crowd of supernumeraries from the triumphal procession.

The second, more intimate, panel recapitulates the actions of the first in reverse order. The final segment of the first gave us the election and Saturninus' betrothal. The second panel begins with Bassianus' lawful seizure of Lavinia, after which Saturninus reenters and accuses Titus of bragging that "I begged the empire at thy hands" (I.i.310). Casting off his patron and renouncing his betrothed, Saturninus takes Tamora for his queen. The stage is now cleared except for Titus himself, who muses on his sudden fall: "Titus, when wert thou wont to walk alone, / Dishonored thus and challenged of wrongs?" (342–343). Titus and Tamora have changed places: his slave has become empress and he is in disgrace.

Shakespeare suggests Titus' stiff-necked pride, his Roman rigidity, when, during the scuffle that follows Bassianus' seizing Lavinia, Titus slays his own son, Mutius, who has taken Bassianus' side. We should note, however, that surprisingly little is made of the killing at this point: Lucius, another son, offers a two-line protest and Titus a two-line reply, after which Mutius is ignored. When Saturninus enters to denounce Titus he does not mention Mutius, although presumably the corpse is lying in full view. What Shakespeare emphasizes is the burial rather than the killing, the opening of the property tomb for Mutius' body in the centerpiece of this panel balancing the earlier funeral of the sons killed in battle. This time the tomb of the heroic Andronici receives a son killed by his own father. The second panel ends with a reprise of the prologue. Once again Saturninus and Bassianus enter, each with his party, from opposite doors; they exchange contentious remarks; and once again a peace, clearly a false one, is arranged.

In this elaborately symmetrical design one item conspicuously lacks a balancing counterpart—the slaughter of Tamora's son. Had he wished, Shakespeare might easily have provided a counterpart in the murder of Mutius, but one of the functions of the design is to direct our attention to the fact that accounts between Titus and Tamora have not been squared. The scene proper ends with the superficially harmonious group exit at line 498, where the Folio mistakenly marks an act division, but Shakespeare's unit is not complete. A long coda follows in which Aaron, who remains onstage while the others exit, is joined by Chiron and Demetrius, and the rape of Lavinia is conceived. The retributive action begins: the slaughter of Tamora's son will find its counterpart in Lavinia's mutilation. The balanced design of the scene thus becomes an emblem of a savage justice in which action begets reaction, atrocity generates atrocity, until equilibrium is restored in universal death.

The tragedy's first movement is concerned with Tamora's revenge, achieved through Aaron. Bassianus is murdered, Titus' sons are made to seem guilty, and Lavinia is raped and mutilated. The movement climaxes in III.i, the central scene.

Tamora's revenge	Central	Titus' revenge
(1022)	scene	(1199)
	(300)	

Initially, the central scene recapitulates the horrors of the first movement. First a formal procession of judges and senators bears Titus' sons to their execution for murder while Titus himself grovels at their feet, vainly pleading for mercy. Next Marcus shows Titus his mutilated daughter. After this Aaron promises to ransom Titus' sons if one of the Andronici will sacrifice his hand. Titus promptly chops off his, but a moment later a messenger brings him his sons' heads and Aaron's offer is revealed as a trick. This final injustice drives Titus mad—he laughs at his sons' heads —and the play pivots as he vows revenge:

> Why, I have not another tear to shed;
> Besides, this sorrow is an enemy,
> And would usurp upon my wat'ry eyes
> And make them blind with tributary tears.
> Then which way shall I find Revenge's cave?
> For these two heads do seem to speak to me,
> And threat me I shall never come to bliss
> Till all these mischiefs be returned again
> Even in their throats that hath committed them.
>   (III.i.266–274)

In a bizarre procession the Andronici exit, Marcus Andronicus carrying one son's head, Titus the other, and Lavinia bringing up the rear with her father's severed hand in her teeth. Two processions thus frame the scene, the judges and senators, representing the wrongs done the Andronici in the name of law, and the injured Andronici themselves, seeking revenge. The latter movement climaxes in the emphatic finale in which Titus banquets Tamora with her sons' flesh, and all the principals are stabbed, after which Lucius, Titus' one remaining son, is chosen emperor. The play thus begins and ends with imperial elections.

In *Titus Andronicus* Shakespeare is in complete control of the overall design. The same is true of *Love's Labor's Lost,* which may have been written about the same time and which in design can be seen as *Titus'* comic counterpart. In recent years, *Love's Labor's* has enjoyed a much higher critical reputation than *Titus,* but this should not blind us to similarities between the plays in structure, especially since *Titus* has perhaps been underrated.

As in *Titus,* Shakespeare experiments here with the very long scene, in this case the finale, which at over 900 lines is the longest single scene in the canon. The scene begins with the ladies, convinced that the amorous gentlemen are jesting, planning their revenge by disguising themselves so that the men will woo the

wrong mistresses. Next the gentlemen enter disguised as Muscovites and the mocking ladies refuse to dance with them. In a play
in which sincerity of feeling and expression is an important issue,
a play in which affected posturing is seen as a kind of mask and
barrier to love, the spectacle of the four disguised couples is delicately symbolic, as is the ladies' refusal to dance. Scoffed off the
stage, the gentlemen quickly return in their own persons, vowing
to woo in a more convincing style:

> O, never will I trust to speeches penned,
> Nor to the motion of a schoolboy's tongue,
> Nor never come in vizard to my friend,
> Nor woo in rime, like a blind harper's song.
> Taffeta phrases, silken terms precise,
> Three-piled hyperboles, spruce affection,
> Figures pedantical—these summer flies
> Have blown me full of maggot ostentation.
> I do forswear them; and I here protest
> By this white glove (how white the hand, God knows)
> Henceforth my wooing mind shall be expressed
> In russet yeas and honest kersey noes.   (V.ii.403–414)

Part of the humor is that Berowne is still wooing in rhyme: the
"old rage" persists, but progress is being made. The next segment is the show of the Nine Worthies presented by Armado,
Holofernes, and the other comic characters, a thematically relevant burlesque of ostentation. In *A Midsummer Night's Dream*
the maturing of the lovers, their passing from one stage of life to
the next, is suggested when they sit with Theseus and Hippolyta
and laugh at Pyramus and Thisbe, the burlesqued images in some
respects of their former selves. In *Love's Labor's Lost* an analogous
change is perhaps suggested when the gentlemen sit with the
ladies and laugh at the show of Worthies. Structurally, this pageant balances the earlier show of Muscovites, the two episodes of
affected play-acting framing the centerpiece in which the ladies
and gentlemen negotiate without masks or disguises. The Worthies pageant explodes when Costard announces that "Hector" has
got Jaquenetta pregnant. A moment later the insulated, artificial
world of the comedy is itself exploded by another intrusion of

"reality" as Marcade arrives with the news that the princess' father is dead. With "honest plain words" the gentlemen again press their suit, and the ladies reply with equal seriousness that the time is too short to "make a world-without-end bargain in." The gentlemen will have to prove their earnestness by passing the year-long tests.

Because of the massive opening of *Titus Andronicus* and the even longer finale of *Love's Labor's*, the editors have had more difficulty than usual in forcing these plays into the alien five-act mold. The *Titus* opening is split into two acts, and the design of *Love's Labor's* is similarly obscured in conventional editions which label the central scene IV.iii and call the entire latter movement Act V. (The long pastoral scene in *The Winter's Tale* also creates difficulties for the editors, which is why the act divisions so badly obscure the design of that play.) As in *Titus,* a simple overall conception of the action enables Shakespeare to articulate *Love's Labor's* very clearly. The first movement is concerned with the academy and the gentlemen's ascetic vows. Everything in this movement looks forward to the central scene in which the impossible vows are openly broken and the academicians at last begin to act like the natural young men they are. The heavily patterned centerpiece, discussed in the second chapter, is the longest scene except for the finale. In it the comedy pivots as the gentlemen discover they are all forsworn and a new triumvirate of "traitors" is formed, the former academicians resolving to lay seige to the ladies in concert. The latter movement is concerned with their amorous assault. As in *Titus,* the play's proportions correspond to its conception:

Initial movement: the academy (1225)	Central scene (381)	Latter movement: open wooing (1061)

The "Lyrical Plays"

A Midsummer Night's Dream, Richard II, and *Romeo and Juliet,* all three probably written around 1595, have long been considered a group on account of the particularly lyrical quality of the verse in each. There are many more specific connections between the plays as well, especially between *A Midsummer Night's Dream* and *Romeo and Juliet.* Bottom's Pyramus and Thisbe play, for instance, is close to Shakespeare's tragedy in theme, and Mercutio's Queen Mab speech echoes the fairy lore of the comedy. In poetry, subtlety, and complexity of thought these three plays represent a clear advance beyond Shakespeare's earlier work, and they are perhaps the first of his plays entitled to be called "great."

A Midsummer Night's Dream is a masterpiece of design. Possibly the massive centerpiece, the forest group, should be connected with Shakespeare's experiments with very long scenes in *Titus* and *Love's Labor's* and with the massive legal centerpiece of *2 Henry VI.* In any case, the fully articulated overall design is the logical result of Shakespeare's impulse to achieve unity by arranging the multiple images of his drama to form a single comprehensive "picture." The play's design is also expressive, for the image of the bright, rational Athens panels surrounding the mysterious and vital centerpiece seems to be intended as an emblematic representation of the structure of the human mind.

The technical problems that Shakespeare faces in *Richard II* are entirely different from those of *A Midsummer Night's Dream.* Here he is concerned with the character and psychology of individuals, and is committed, moreover, to remain more or less faithful to the outlines of history. Nevertheless, in its own fashion, *Richard II* is equally impressive in design. One mark of Shakespeare's success is that there is no ambiguity about the basic structure, which rests upon the opposition of two antithetical characters, Richard and Bolingbroke. Indeed, it is commonplace to point out the play's symmetrical pattern, and to cite Richard's image of two buckets, one rising, one falling, as an emblem for the overall design. Nor is there much ambiguity about the turning point. The play pivots in the the Flint Castle scene (III.iii) in which Richard appears upon the walls to confront his rebellious subject, and then with self-conscious histrionics turns his descent to the main platform into a symbolic act:

Down, down I come, like glist'ring Phaeton,
Wanting the manage of unruly jades.
In the base Court? Base court, where kings grow base,
To come at traitors' calls and do them grace!
In the base court come down? Down court! down king!
For night owls shriek where mounting larks should sing.
                                        (III.iii.178–183)

In the first movement Richard is dominant, in the second, Boling-broke.

The Flint Castle scene is part of a larger group. *Richard II* opens, we recall, with a group in which two formal, public scenes dealing with the chivalric contest between Bolingbroke and Mowbray frame the intimate conversation between Gaunt and his grieving sister, the Duchess of Gloucester, whose husband Richard has murdered. The play's latter movement begins with a similar group. Once again a pair of formal, ceremonious scenes—Flint Castle and the deposition scene (IV.i)—frame an intimate scene concerned with a grieving lady. This time, however, the lady is Richard's own queen, mourning with her ladies-in-waiting over her husband's misfortunes (III.iv). As in the first group, the centerpiece provides information necessary to understand the public side panels, the overheard conversation between the gardener and his man about the analogy between gardens and commonwealths serving as a gloss on Richard's decline. Corresponding scenes in the two groups are roughly equivalent in length:

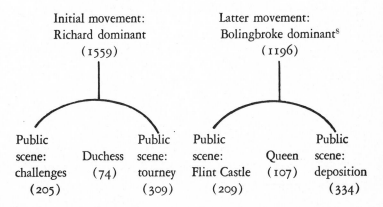

Initial movement:
Richard dominant
(1559)

Latter movement:
Bolingbroke dominant[8]
(1196)

Public
scene:
challenges
(205)

Duchess
(74)

Public
scene:
tourney
(309)

Public
scene:
Flint Castle
(209)

Queen
(107)

Public
scene:
deposition
(334)

The two pairs of public scenes are the only ones in the play in which Richard and Bolingbroke appear together. Furthermore, the deposition scene explicitly recalls the earlier group. It begins with Bagot formally accusing Aumerle of complicity in Gloucester's death, after which a series of nobles throw down their gages, challenging the accused. This time, however, it is Bolingbroke rather than Richard who presides over the challenges.

Structurally, *Richard II* looks forward to *Hamlet* in that the initial movement is further articulated into two distinct phases. In fact, the initial movement is designed exactly as if it were a short play in its own right. The first phase, consisting of four scenes (I.i-iv), is concerned with Bolingbroke's banishment and Richard's departure for Ireland. The second, consisting of five scenes (II.ii-III.ii), is concerned with returns, Bolingbroke's return from exile and Richard's from Ireland. The centerpiece is the long scene devoted to John of Gaunt's death (II.i), which marks the end of an era.

Initial phase: departures	Death of Gaunt	Latter phase: returns
(653)	(300)	(606)

It is significant that the news of Gaunt's sickness comes immediately after Richard decides to farm the realm (I.iv), and that the first word of Bolingbroke's illegal return, the birth of the new era, comes a few moments after his father's death.

The death scene is very carefully designed. It begins with Gaunt and his brother, York, discussing Richard's mismanagement of the realm, a subject which leads to Gaunt's prophetic speech in praise of England. This private segment is balanced at the end of the scene by the conversation in which Northumberland, Willoughby, and Ross again rehearse the story of Richard's misbehavior, after which Northumberland reveals that Bolingbroke is returning. Structurally, this momentous news corresponds to Gaunt's prophecies in the first segment. The two private segments frame the centerpiece in which the king and queen with many courtiers in their train dominate the scene.

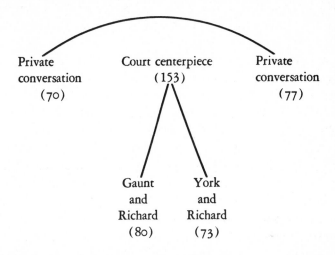

In the first part of the centerpiece, Gaunt confronts Richard with his failings, after which he is borne offstage to die. In the second part, Richard seizes the Lancaster estates, an act which provokes even mild York to vigorous protest. It is in the exact center of the scene, we should note, that Northumberland announces that Gaunt's tongue is a stringless instrument: "Words, life, and all, old Lancaster hath spent" (II.i.150).

Like Duke Humphrey in *2 Henry VI*, Gaunt is what we can call a "structural character." His death punctuates a crucial point in the design. Shakespeare employs structural characters a number of times, and when he does the characters generally tend to be symbolic, although not necessarily so bluntly symbolic as Humphrey and Gaunt. For instance, Old Adam—surely, his name is meant to be suggestive—appears in the first movement of *As You Like It* but not in the second.[9] In a similar fashion, Lear's fool disappears mysteriously after the centerpiece of the tragedy. Likewise, Mercutio, whose name is also suggestive, helps to articulate the design of *Romeo and Juliet*.

Like *Richard II*, *Romeo and Juliet* bears witness to Shakespeare's growing architectonic powers. The design of this play, based on the normal two-movement pattern, is both clear and expressive. The initial movement, concerned with the growth of love, is comic in tone; the latter movement is tragic. Built into the overall design is thus the motif of sport turning serious which informs so many aspects of the play. Romeo, playing at love, acting the role of the conventional, despairing worshipper of cruel beauty, suddenly finds himself loving in earnest. Mercutio, meaning merely to teach an affected bully a lesson, is mortally wounded. Again and again, characters find themselves out of their depths, discover that seemingly straightforward situations are neither straightforward nor within their control. Capulet thinks he understands how to guarantee a comfortable future for his daughter. Friar Laurence thinks he sees a ready and easy way to reconcile Capulets and Montagues without further bloodletting. The motif is introduced in the opening episode in which Sampson and Gregory, high-spirited and heedless of consequences, pick a fight with Montague's servants.

The opening, central scene, and finale are all "big" scenes, requiring perhaps as many as 20 or 25 actors and supernumeraries. One other scene, the Capulet ball, makes comparable demands on the company, but the three "pillars" are the only scenes in which the prince, the formal representative of authority, appears.

Comic movement	Central	Tragic movement
(1346)	scene	(1423)
	(195)	

The central scene and turning point is III.i, the scene in which Mercutio and Tybalt are killed and Romeo banished. This begins with an echo of the opening as two characters again stroll across the stage discussing the Capulet-Montague feud:

> I pray thee, good Mercutio, let's retire.
> The day is hot, the Capulets abroad,
> And, if we meet, we shall not 'scape a brawl,
> For now, these hot days, is the mad blood stirring.   (1-4)

Like the servants of the opening, Mercutio is itching for a fight, and it soon comes, playfulness turning deadly serious as he is slain under Romeo's arm. In the emphatic central position, framed by the slaying of Mercutio on one side and the murder of Tybalt on the other, Shakespeare gives us a speaking picture of a young man caught in a tragic dilemma:

> This gentleman, the Prince's near ally,
> My very friend, hath got this mortal hurt
> In my behalf—my reputation stained
> With Tybalt's slander—Tybalt, that an hour
> Hath been my cousin. O sweet Juliet,
> Thy beauty hath made me effeminate
> And in my temper soft'ned valor's steel!   (107–113)

A moment later Benvolio reports Mercutio's death, and Romeo makes his decision: "This day's black fate on moe days doth depend; / This but begins the woe others must end" (117–118). Perfectly balanced on either side of the pivotal centerpiece are the two lovers' scenes discussed in the third chapter; forming a large, pathetic diptych, they frame the center of the play.

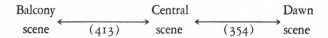

| Balcony | Central | Dawn |
| scene ←——— (413) ———→ | scene ←——— (354) ———→ | scene |

In each of these scenes, we recall, sunrise is an image for the threatening reality the lovers fear. Between the two scenes in symbolic half-light Shakespeare places the central picture of noon's hot glare.

   Much as he did in *Richard II,* Shakespeare divides the initial movement of *Romeo and Juliet* into two roughly equal phases, separated by the brief Chorus. (This Chorus contributes nothing to the narrative or theme. Its function is purely structural.) The first phase climaxes with the ball at which Romeo and Juliet meet, a major scene for which the audience is prepared well in advance. The second phase, which begins with the balcony scene, prepares for another major event, the lovers' wedding in Friar Laurence's cell, which is signalled in advance as if it is to be the turning point of the play. When the marriage scene arrives, however, it turns out to be remarkably short and unclimactic, running only 37 lines. Immediately, we are rushed on to the real turning point, the tragic double slaying, which comes with almost as much of a shock to us as it does to the characters involved. This strategy looks forward to the opening of *Macbeth,* where pacing is also used, as we have seen, to recreate in the audience something like the protagonist's experience.

The story of Romeo and Juliet was well known long before Shakespeare wrote his tragedy, for it had been told and retold by the Italian and French romancers, and there also seems to have been an earlier English play on the subject. Shakespeare may have known several versions, but in the actual process of composition he almost certainly relied on one alone, Arthur Brooke's long narrative poem, published in 1562, *The Tragicall Historye of Romeus and Iuliet.* In adapting Brooke's poem, Shakespeare compressed the time scheme from nine months to a few days, greatly increasing the speed of the action. Mercutio he created from a brief hint in the poem, and he reduced Juliet's age from 16 to not quite 14, thus emphasizing the lovers' youth. With only a very few changes, however, he followed the narrative exactly as he found it in Brooke. Indeed, the poem and the play are so similar in this respect that it is often said that Shakespeare found the structure of his tragedy ready made.[10]

But discussions of the relationship between Brooke's poem and Shakespeare's play do not take design into account. The narrative is Brooke's, but the shaping pattern is wholly Shakespeare's. The opening brawl, for instance, the first "pillar" of the structure, is developed from what in Brooke is merely exposition (ll.30–50). Brooke's narrative begins with Romeo, and his first real "scene" is the Capulet ball (ll. 153–362). Especially revealing is the fact that the material that becomes Shakespeare's central scene (ll. 955–1072) falls nowhere near the middle of the 3,000-line poem. Shakespeare, in other words, completely reworked the proportions of the narrative.

He also made one major change in the narrative sequence. Brooke gives separate descriptions of the lovers' wedding night (ll. 827–930) and their last night together before Romeo's exile (ll. 1527–1718). The wedding night in the poem comes before the turning point, the fateful slaying of Tybalt. Shakespeare combined the two episodes in the dawn scene (III.v), delaying the wedding night until after the murder and sentence of exile. Plainly he wanted to tighten the story and increase the pathos of Romeo and Juliet's one moment of union. But evidently he also had in mind the balance of the two lovers' scenes, one on either side of the centerpiece. This naturally has no equivalent in Brooke. Moreover, in order to make the scenes parallel in design he had to do considerable reshaping. There is no precedent in the poem for the Mercutio-Benvolio segment before the balcony episode. And to create the corresponding "outsiders" segment for the dawn scene he had to edit out the long description of Romeo in Mantua (ll. 1719–1780), which Brooke placed between his treatment of the lovers' last night and his description of Juliet's conflict with her parents (ll. 1781–2004).

We should note that, because of the radical shift in the wedding night's position, the turning point in the play ought to come even earlier than it does in the poem. The principal reason it does not is Shakespeare's expansion of Brooke's few lines of exposition into the first of the play's "pillars." He also moved up the introduction of Paris and expanded a brief mention of Capulet sending around invitations (l. 162) into the second scene. The third scene, which introduces Juliet, has no precedent at this point in the poem. These expansions of the early part of the narrative delay the turning point and allow Shakespeare to use Brooke's first "scene," the Capulet ball, as the climax of the play's opening phase.

The informing motif of sport turning serious is of course Shakespeare's own. He may have taken a hint for his opening episode from Brooke's passing reference to the little spark which kindles a great fire (l. 35), but the brawl, so far as it is described in the poem, is a blood-bath without levity. Shakespeare used the motif to define the two movements, creating a "structural character," Mercutio, in part to establish the initially comic tone. In shaping his play, then, Shakespeare found not only form but meaning, an expressive pattern which helped to give the narrative significance. He did much more than merely condense Brooke's lumbering poem and translate its rough poulter's measure into his own sweetest style.

6

The Later Plays

Julius Caesar and *Troilus and Cressida*

In the two early tragedies, *Titus Andronicus* and *Romeo and Juliet,* the central scenes, while clearly marked, are really little more than turning points in the narrative. Whatever sense of special significance these scenes project derives largely from the fact that, as turning points, they naturally reflect in little the over-all narrative structure of the plays—the revenge for revenge pattern of *Titus* and the sport turning serious pattern of *Romeo and Juliet.* In the later tragedies the central scenes are fashioned more on the model of *2 Henry VI,* that is, they do not merely mirror narrative patterns but provide symbolic tableaux. The play's pivot becomes an allegorical core as well. Having mastered his form, Shakespeare is laboring to load every rift with ore, trying to generate as high a charge of felt significance as possible. In the heart of the play he wishes to locate also the heart of the mystery.

In *Julius Caesar* we can see the tendency to exert more and more pressure on the centerpiece beginning. Like *Hamlet, Julius Caesar* has an unusually long prologue, the scene in which Flavius and Marullus berate the celebrating plebeians. This functions some-what like the old dumb show common some years earlier, fore-shadowing the main action without giving it away completely.[1] The opening scene proper (I.ii) begins with Caesar's triumphal procession and the soothsayer's warning to beware the ides of March, after which Cassius and Brutus are left alone onstage. (Here, as in *Antony and Cleopatra,* Shakespeare uses the formal procession as a "classical" equivalent for the usual court opening.)

This is a long and, as we would expect, a highly wrought scene, but its internal organization need not concern us here. The central scene is the assassination (III.i), which comes exactly in the center of the play, dividing it into two movements, the conspirators' action and Antony's counter-action. Beginning with another formal procession and another warning from the soothsayer, the assassination scene echoes the opening. This scene, too, is highly wrought. We may note, for example, that Antony's entrance comes in the center, dividing the scene into two equal segments, the first concerned with the murder and the second initiating the revenge action of the latter movement. Caesar's death comes in the center of the first segment.

In the middle of the central scene of *Romeo and Juliet* Shakespeare for an instant halted the action to give us a picture of Romeo at the turning point of his life, trapped by the conflicting claims of love and honor. In *Julius Caesar* there is a similar but much more emphatic pause at the crisis. Immediately after the murder the conspirators stoop and bathe their hands in Caesar's blood—the dramatic irony of this ritual purification is obvious and effective—and Shakespeare suddenly draws upon a version of the all-the-world's-a-stage metaphor to freeze the action and imprint the tableau upon our imaginations.

> *Cassius.* Stoop then and wash. How many ages hence
> Shall this our lofty scene be acted over
> In states unborn and accents yet unknown!
> *Brutus.* How many times shall Caesar bleed in sport,
> That now on Pompey's basis lies along
> No worthier than the dust!
> *Cassius.* So oft as that shall be,
> So often shall the knot of us be called
> The men that gave their country liberty. (III.i.111–118)

We who are watching Brutus and Cassius kneeling know that the consequences of the assassination will not be what they suppose. The dramatic metaphor collapses time so that, like gods, we see past, present, and future, intentions and consequences, implicit in a moment, and the picture of the conspirators confidently bathing in Caesar's blood emerges as an emblem of the tragedy's central mystery.

In the centerpiece of *Troilus and Cressida* Shakespeare employs the same technique for the same effect. Two scenes stand at the center of this play, III.ii, in which Troilus and Cressida are at last brought together, and III.iii, which brings about the abrupt reversal of fortune as Agamemnon agrees to exchange Antenor for Cressida. The first of these, III.ii, concludes with a time-collapsing tableau very similar to that of *Julius Caesar*. Troilus takes his mistress's hand and pledges that "true as Troilus" will be a motto for eternity, to which Cressida replies that "false as Cressid" will be her motto if she proves inconstant. Stepping between the two, Pandarus seals the bargain and completes the ironic tableau:

> Here I hold your hand, here my cousin's. If ever you prove false one to another, since I have taken such pains to bring you together, let all pitiful goers-between be called to the world's end after my name; call them all Pandars; let all constant men be Troiluses, all false women Cressids, and all brokers-between Pandars! (III.ii.190–196)

The tableau harks back to the opening scene and Troilus' request for an oracle to reveal "What Cressid is, what Pandar, and what we" (I.i.95). In fact, the "what is" theme, as we may call it, that is, the concern with identity and value and the meaning behind a famous name such as Helen or Agamemnon, dominates practically every scene in the first movement. The centerpiece is the climax, the moment when this theme becomes entirely clear, and in the ironic tableau Shakespeare begins the transition to the dominant theme of the second movement, the theme that will answer the questions posed in the first—time.[2]

The technique that gives special significance to the centerpieces in *Julius Caesar* and *Troilus and Cressida* is analogous in many ways to that employed in a number of modern films, the abrupt freezing of the action at a single frame, held for a few moments until it becomes a kind of emblem, after which the film proceeds as before. The dramatic illusion is purposely shattered and the play, or film, calls attention to itself as a work of art. The use of artistic self-consciousness in the centerpiece links these two plays with *Hamlet,* where the stage metaphor is fully realized in the central scene, the mousetrap. The three plays are also closely associated in date, all probably written sometime around the turn of the century. Shakespeare's next tragedy is very likely *Othello,* and here he uses a somewhat different technique for emphasizing the centerpiece, one which associates this play with *Lear.*

Othello and *Lear*

As A. C. Bradley pointed out, the narrative structure of *Othello* is exceptional among the tragedies in that the main conflict does not begin in earnest until the second half of the play. The result is that the latter movement is more exciting than the first, whereas the reverse is normally the case.[3] This is true and important; nevertheless, the design of *Othello* is perfectly regular. In lieu of a single opening scene, the first of the three "pillars," we have, as we have seen, a highly organized group, the three Venice scenes. The third pillar, the finale, is also massive, running about 400 lines. In the center, dividing the play into roughly equal movements, is the temptation scene (III.iii) in which Othello's jealousy is born. This scene, in which we watch Othello gradually transformed, is one of the most dynamic in Shakespeare, and, with its obvious psychological interest, perhaps represents his closest approach to our own fluid literary mode. Yet, of course, its modernity is more apparent than real.

The temptation scene begins cheerfully with Desdemona promising to help Cassio recover his standing with Othello. Confident of Cassio's fundamental decency and her husband's fairness, Desdemona does not doubt that she can arrange a reconciliation. Seeing Othello enter, Cassio discreetly withdraws, and the tone of tne scene suddenly changes as Iago, in a brief, whispered exchange, plants the seed of Othello's destruction:

> *Iago.* Ha! I like not that.
> *Othello.* What dost thou say?
> *Iago.* Nothing, my lord; or if—I know not what.
> *Othello.* Was not that Cassio parted from my wife?
> *Iago.* Cassio, my lord? No, sure, I cannot think it,

> That he would steal away so guilty-like,
> Seeing your coming.
> *Othello.*   I do believe 'twas he.   (III.iii.35–40)

With easy grace, Desdemona reminds her husband of Cassio's worth and asks for his pardon, but Othello, his mind on Iago's exclamation, is somewhat distracted and irritable. As soon as Desdemona exits, however, he shakes himself free from his darker thoughts: "Excellent wretch! Perdition catch my soul / But I do love thee! and when I love thee not, / Chaos is come again" (90–92). This speech, summarizing Othello's present state of mind and foreshadowing the future, marks the end of the first segment, which serves as a prologue to the scene proper.

Left alone with Othello, Iago begins to work in earnest, cultivating the Moor's suspicions with hints and innuendos, reminding him that Desdemona deceived her father, and leading him to the conclusion that it is only logical to suppose she has deceived him as well. Othello's soliloquy, summarizing his changed attitude toward his wife, punctuates the end of this long segment: "If I do prove her haggard, / Though that her jesses were my dear heartstrings, / I'd whistle her off and let her down the wind / To prey at fortune" (260–263). The Moor is now in the early stages of jealousy, aroused but still capable of reason and doubt.

The first Iago-Othello segment is balanced by another of about the same length at the end of the scene, introduced by the short soliloquy in which Iago describes how the Moor is changing under the influence of his poison. These two Iago-Othello conversations frame the centerpiece, which dramatizes symbolically the passage of Othello's love, his marriage, and his life, from Desdemona's hands into Iago's.

| Prologue (92) | Iago and Othello (165) | Othello alone (20) | Centerpiece: the handkerchief (43) | Iago alone (13) | Iago and Othello (147) |

The crucial symbol in *Othello* is the handkerchief with magic in its web, which figures prominently here for the first time in the play. Desdemona enters and Othello, implicitly referring to the cuckold's horns, complains of a pain upon his forehead. She offers to bind his head with the handkerchief, but he angrily pushes it away: "Your napkin is too little" (287). Leaving the handkerchief on the stage, Othello and Desdemona exit. In the middle of the centerpiece Emilia retrieves it and comments on its importance:

> This was her first remembrance from the Moor,
> My wayward husband hath a hundred times
> Wooed me to steal it; but she so loves the token
> (For he conjured her she should ever keep it)
> That she reserves it evermore about her
> To kiss and talk to.   (291–296)

Immediately, Iago enters and pounces on the napkin. Every movement, every gesture, in the centerpiece is significant. Indeed, the actions count more than the words, and the entire episode might almost be played in pantomime. Shakespeare incorporates the heart of the mystery in a dumb show that is also the turning point of the tragedy.

Iago's soliloquy after the handkerchief episode prepares us for a transformed Othello:

> Look where he comes! Not poppy nor mandragora,
> Nor all the drowsy syrups of the world,
> Shall ever med'cine thee to that sweet sleep
> Which thou owedst yesterday.   (330–333)

The Moor is now utterly distraught, and Iago binds his victim to him. The scene ends with a tableau, the picture of Iago and Othello kneeling in mutual vows, and a subtle return of the subject with which it opened, the lieutenancy: "Now art thou my lieutenant." "I am your own for ever" (479–480), Iago replies, but what he means is that Othello is *his* forever. In this phrase we have the clue to one of the temptation scene's sources of power. The ultimate provenance of the scene is to be found in the morality plays with their many similar scenes of temptation and fall, and hovering about Iago throughout the episode is a certain diabolic glow lending extra meaning to such words as "perdition" and "bound." We have not exactly witnessed the fall of mankind from faith, but we have seen something more than a domestic misunderstanding.

King Lear is another play concerned with love and hate, and here again Shakespeare draws heavily on the morality mode to help universalize the story of the proud, short-sighted king who chooses badly, is humbled and reborn, and is reunited with the angelic daughter he rejected. Again the turning point is a psychic transformation, and again Shakespeare locates a crucial symbol in the center of the play. Indeed, in *Lear* the entire centerpiece becomes emblematic, the storm on the heath being as much an expanded metaphor as the midnight forest of love in *A Midsummer Night's Dream*.

The heath group begins with a prologue, the brief scene in which an unnamed gentleman draws a verbal portrait of the king in the storm: "Contending with the fretful elements; / Bids the wind blow the earth into the sea, / Or swell the curled waters 'bove the main, / That things might change or cease" (III.i.4–7). The group proper consists of five symmetrically arranged scenes, three major panels which show Lear's increasing madness and two minor panels concerned with the Gloucester subplot.

III.i	III.ii	III.iii	III.iv	III.v	III.vi[4]
prologue	Lear	subplot	Lear	subplot	Lear
(55)	(95)	(23)	(175)	(24)	(113)

As in the *Othello* centerpiece, where Shakespeare's technique for portraying gradual psychological change is to give us pictures of Othello in progressive stages of passion, so here he gives us in rapid succession pictures of the stages of madness. In the first Lear panel, which begins with the famous "Blow, winds, and crack your cheeks," we see a man in the extreme of passion but still sane. In the central panel the long foreseen madness arrives. Lear begins the scene speaking rationally of the tempest in his mind, but after Edgar's entrance as Tom o' Bedlam his remarks become progressively more disordered, and Kent sums up what we have witnessed, "His wits begin t'unsettle" (III.iv.153). In the final panel Lear arraigns the joint-stools, thinking them his daughters. He is now completely mad, and once again Kent defines the situation for us: "His wits are gone" (III.vi.85).

The dominant theme of the first Lear panel is injustice. Lear contrasts the elements' cruelty with that of his daughters: "I tax you not, you elements, with unkindness. / I never gave you kingdom, called you children; / You owe me no subscription" (III.ii.-16–18). His fury, mirrored in the storm, climaxes as he calls upon the gods to find out their true enemies, the secret scheming criminals who escape just punishment.

>   Tremble, thou wretch,
> That hast within thee undivulged crimes
> Unwhipped of justice. Hide thee, thou bloody hand,
> Thou perjured, and thou simular of virtue
> That art incestuous. Caitiff, to pieces shake,
> That under covert and convenient seeming
> Has practiced on man's life. Close pent-up guilts,
> Rive your concealing continents and cry
> These dreadful summoners grace. I am a man
> More sinned against than sinning.   (III.ii.51–60)

This panel is balanced by the final Lear scene, which returns to the fierce satiric mode as Lear madly believes that he is righting the world's wrongs, arraigning his daughters before the bar of justice.

The central panel, the longest scene in the group, is the play's turning point. Beginning with the opening scene, in which Lear divests himself of his power and his one loving daughter, the principal action of the initial movement has been the progressive "exposure" of the king. Literally and metaphorically, stripped of all the "superfluities," all that is not required to ᴜ tain physical life. Honor, dignity, love—everything that is implied in the key word "service," everything that distinguishes civilization from savagery, man from beast, Goneril and Regan tear from him. Almost before our eyes they shrink his retinue of a hundred knights to fifty, twenty-five, five, and none, deciding that their father has no need of servants. "O reason not the need!" Lear protests. "Our basest beggars / Are in the poorest thing superfluous. / Allow not nature more than nature needs, / Man's life is cheap as beast's" (II.iv.259–262). This stripping action climaxes in the emblematic tableau in the middle of the central panel in which Lear stands face to face with the thing itself, unaccommodated man, and in a sympathetic gesture tears the "lendings" from his own body. Paradoxically, it is in his vision of the subhuman, in his contemplation of this mirror of his own degradation, that Lear begins to find his own humanity. Humbly admitting his ignorance, Lear addresses Tom o' Bedlam with profound respect as "noble philosopher," and at the end of the scene the two exit together in a pairing that recalls by contrast his earlier exit arm in arm with Burgundy. The king has become the beggar's disciple.

The two minor panels dealing with the subplot are arranged on either side of the centerpiece and conceived in such a way that the subplot's turning point, Gloucester's decision to aid the king regardless of consequences, coincides with that of the main plot. The minor panels provide an ironic counterpoint to the Lear scenes, illustrating the dangers of exercising pity and charity in a wicked world. The first (III.iii) shows Gloucester telling Edmund that he can no longer bear the sisters' unnatural dealing and that, together, they must help the king. In the second (III.v) Edmund betrays his father to Cornwall, receiving the earldom as his reward. The crucial moment comes in the central Lear panel. Immediately following Lear's contemplation of unaccommodated man, Gloucester, having made his choice of sides, enters carrying a torch. "Look, here comes a walking fire" (III.iv.107), the fool

arrival. Into the darkness and cold of the
little warmth.

Macbeth

ath scenes Shakespeare perhaps had taken the em-
phatic centerpiece as far as it could go in tragedy. *Macbeth* is in
some respects a departure in design from *Hamlet, Othello,* and
Lear. For one thing, the center receives nothing like the emphasis
it does in the other tragedies. For another, *Hamlet, Othello,* and
Lear are built in large, highly designed units, with scenes that
often run 400 or more lines. In *Macbeth* Shakespeare seems to
be experimenting with the speed and flexibility of many short
scenes. There are only two long scenes in the play, the eighth
(II.i-iii), showing the murder of Duncan, and the eighteenth
(IV.iii), the England scene. In its own way, however, *Macbeth*
is perhaps the most elaborately designed of all the tragedies.

Macbeth is the history of a man who willfully and consciously
undertakes an act that cuts him off forever from personal repose
or social communion. We recall that in the murder scene Macbeth refers to the sleep he has murdered as "great nature's second
course, / Chief nourisher in life's feast" (II.ii.38–39). Feasting
is this play's metaphor for social harmony, and in the center, the
banquet scene (III.iv), the image of life's feast is concretely realized. In murdering Banquo—possibly a pun is intended in his
name—Macbeth has excluded himself from the banquet of life.
He is barred from the table by the image of his own tyranny, the
gory figure of the man he has slain.

The banquet scene divides the tragedy into the normal two
movements, running 1,017 and 952 lines respectively. The initial
movement is a steady rising action, Macbeth achieving and con-
solidating his power as he murders first Duncan and then Banquo.
After the appearance of the ghost, however, Macbeth is on the
defensive, and the counter-action begins to develop with the news
that Macduff is in England, raising a power to overthrow the tyrant. Banquo, the man who does not fall, is the principal foil to

Macbeth in the initial movement; in the second movement, his foil is the patriotic Macduff. The division into two movements is also marked by the reappearance of the witches immediately after the banquet, a structural device analogous to the reappearance of the ghost soon after the mousetrap scene in *Hamlet*.[5]

Yet the banquet scene, luminous as it is, runs only 144 lines, and, as a turning point, it is less important than the murder of Duncan, which makes Macbeth king, or the England scene, which begins his overthrow. Looking at the play from a slightly different angle now, we can see that superimposed upon the usual two-movement structure is a second pattern, an extension of the principle of organization we noticed in *Richard II,* where in the center of the first movement we found the pivotal, emblematic, death of Gaunt. In *Macbeth,* each movement has its own center-piece, the murder scene coming just in the center of the first and the England scene in the second. As the only long scenes in the play, these two stand out from all the others, the murder running 279 lines and the England scene 240.

The two scenes are also parallel in design, the structure of the second perhaps being intended to echo that of the first. The murder scene, we recall, consists of three segments: the night panel, a long crescendo of fear, which climaxes in the portentous knocking; the brief emblematic central panel, the porter; and the dawn panel, the long discovery action as the household is roused. The three segments of the England scene are roughly analogous. The scene begins with the conversation in which Malcolm, testing Macduff, makes himself out to be a moral monster. The central panel, like the porter episode, brings on a minor, symbolic character, a doctor, who describes the English king's holiness and miraculous healing powers, a subject Malcolm expounds further:

> *Macduff.* What's the disease he means?
> *Malcolm.* 'Tis called the evil.
>   A most miraculous work in this good King,
>   Which often since my here-remain in England
>   I have seen him do: how he solicits heaven
>   Himself best knows, but strangely-visited people,
>   All swol'n and ulcerous, pitiful to the eye,

The mere despair of surgery, he cures,
Hanging a golden stamp about their necks,
Put on with holy prayers; and 'tis spoken,
To the succeeding royalty he leaves
The healing benediction. With this strange virtue,
He hath a heavenly gift of prophecy,
And sundry blessings hang about his throne
That speak him full of grace.   (IV.iii.146–159)

The third segment, like that of the murder scene, is a discovery action. Ross arrives with news of the murder of Macduff's wife and children, and this leads to the decision to invade Scotland from England. The scene as a whole thus resolves itself into two dark panels framing a gleaming emblematic centerpiece, the picture of holy King Edward dispensing health. This centerpiece emphatically establishes the health-disease motif of the tragedy's final phase, which begins with an image of Scotland's sickness, the sleep-walking scene, a portrait of a mind diseased. In the final phase, Malcolm and Macduff in effect carry the health of England back to Scotland.

The murder and England scenes, symmetrically disposed on either side of the play, define a large triadic design reminiscent of *A Midsummer Night's Dream* in which two daylight panels frame the extended nighttime centerpiece. The framing panels in *Macbeth* are the initial fall in which Scotland passes into the tyrant's grasp, and the final redemption, Macbeth's overthrow. In the center is the portrait of tyranny in action, Scotland's dark night of fear. I use the terms "fall" and "redemption," with their theological overtones, deliberately, for much of the special richness of *Macbeth,* like *Othello* and *Lear,* derives from the way it reverberates with more than secular meaning. The two long pivotal scenes provide in effect a great diptych of fear and hope, a lurid, fiery panel in the porter episode, and in the England scene a shining vision of all that is desirable, the portrait of a holy, life-giving —and unseen—king. Between these two panels comes the extended centerpiece, the picture of Scotland fallen and suffering, waiting for redemption.

Antony and Cleopatra

Macbeth is an experiment in the use of many short scenes for speed, flexibility, and rapid juxtapositions. *Antony and Cleopatra,* with 36 scenes in some 3,000 lines, carries the experiment further. In other respects as well, as we shall see, the design of this play seems to be the logical extension of *Macbeth.*

The short first scene of *Antony and Cleopatra* is a masterpiece of economy, a brilliant example of the principles of Shakespearean design reduced to their simplest and most elegant terms. The ancestor of this scene is perhaps the *Lear* opening, in which Shakespeare uses the frame pattern to distinguish dramatically between the public and private spheres of life. Here Shakespeare uses it to establish the opposition between the Roman and Egyptian perspectives on life.

Demetrius and Philo, two Roman soldiers, provide the frame, commenting upon Antony before the procession enters, and then remaining to comment again after it has departed. Like an old-fashioned Presenter, Philo interprets the central panel for us in advance, describing how Antony has debased himself: "Take but good note, and you shall see in him / The triple pillar of the world transformed / Into a strumpet's fool. Behold and see" (I.i.11–13). From the Roman point of view, Philo is undoubtedly right, Antony is a sorry figure. But the Egyptian centerpiece is designed to contradict the Roman frame point for point, or rather, to reverse the perspective of the frame, suggesting an alternative interpretation of Antony's state. According to Philo, when love— he calls it "dotage"—overflows the measure it becomes slavery. But according to Antony, there is beggary in love that can be measured. Philo sees Antony's staying in Egypt as a sign of servitude, but Cleopatra, ironically urging Antony to hear the messengers, suggests with equal plausibility that it is in Rome that Antony is a servant. Philo has a Roman soldier's view of the good life: when Antony's eyes "glowed like plated Mars" on the battlefield, then he was noble. But Antony rejects the pursuit of empire as unworthy—kingdoms are clay—and proclaims that the "nobleness of life" is to live as he and Cleopatra do in Egypt. Being irreconcilable, and equally convincing, the perspectives of the frame and centerpiece vibrate endlessly in our minds. The scene as a whole is contrived to provide a completely ambiguous view of Antony.[6]

The design of the second scene is also based on the Rome-Egypt opposition. It begins with a very Egyptian episode, Cleopatra's household at play, the ladies-in-waiting having their fortunes read by a soothsayer. This panel is a picture of idleness and bawdry, with perhaps a hint of genial brothel atmosphere in its pervasive sexuality: in general, it tends to confirm the Roman view of Egyptian frivolity. The latter part of the scene is a Roman panel, filled with bustle and activity as messengers bring Antony news from all parts of the Empire. Each in its own fashion, the Egyptian and Roman panels are both concerned with the future, the Egyptian with such matters as lovers, children, and length of life; the Roman with state affairs and death—Fulvia's death, Pompey's growing power, and what all this means to Antony and to the future of the Empire. The bearer of tidings in the Egyptian panel is the soothsayer; his equivalent in the Roman panel is the series of messengers. This subtle parallel, the contrast between the magical seer and the matter-of-fact messengers, helps to suggest another aspect of the Egypt-Rome opposition, lending resonance to Antony's Roman vow, "I must from this enchanting queen break off" (I.ii.124).

Significantly, the only character who appears in both the Egyptian and the Roman panels is the amphibious Enobarbus, the man who believes, at least for a time, in never giving all the heart and who therefore can pass freely between Egypt and Rome, unaffected by either. Significantly, too, Cleopatra, whom we might expect to be the epitome of idleness, takes no part in her ladies' sport. Placed between the two panels, her brief appearance forms the pivot on which the scene turns:

> *Cleopatra.* Saw you my lord?
> *Enobarbus.* No, lady.
> *Cleopatra.* Was he not here?

Charmian.   No, madam.
Cleopatra.   He was disposed to mirth; but on the sudden
    A Roman thought hath struck him. Enobarbus!
Enobarbus.   Madam?
Cleopatra.   Seek him, and bring him hither. Where's Alexas?
Alexas.   Here at your service. My lord approaches.
    Enter Antony with a Messenger {and Attendants}
Cleopatra.   We will not look upon him. Go with us.
                                                    (I.ii.76–83)

Conducting her amorous business with Roman curtness, if not
with Roman consistency, Cleopatra is as brisk and vigorous as
Antony himself in the latter panel. Just as the opening scene gives
us an ambiguous view of Antony, the second scene is designed to
dispose of any simplistic ideas we may have about Cleopatra.

In case we have missed the point about the Egyptian queen,
Shakespeare repeats it in the third scene, which shows the lovers'
parting as Antony leaves for Rome. Again, Cleopatra enters
briskly, speaking in abrupt, energetic phrases.

Cleopatra.   Where is he?
Charmian.   I did not see him since.
Cleopatra.   See where he is, who's with him, what he does:
    I did not send you. If you find him sad,
    Say I am dancing; if in mirth, report
    That I am sudden sick. Quick, and return.   (I.iii.1–5)

When Antony enters, Cleopatra reads his looks and decides to be
sick and sullen: her famous Egyptian languor is play-acting, another device of a woman cunning past man's thought. The point
is summed up at the end of the scene. "But that your royalty /
Holds idleness your subject, I should take you / For idleness itself," Antony says, to which Cleopatra replies that such idleness
as hers is "sweating labor" (I.iii.91–93).

We can see now that Shakespeare's solution to the technical
challenge of composing in short scenes is the same in *Antony and
Cleopatra* as in *Macbeth*. Once again the opening phase is organized in several patterned groups, analogous in function to the
long scenes of *Hamlet* or *Othello*.

The first three scenes, corresponding to the field group in *Macbeth,* are all concerned with the Egypt-Rome opposition and particularly with the thematic contrast between idleness and activity. The two brief scenes that show Antony and Cleopatra together frame the much longer second scene with its contrasted Egyptian and Roman panels.

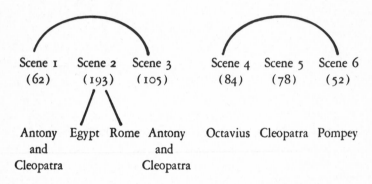

Scene 1	Scene 2	Scene 3		Scene 4	Scene 5	Scene 6
(62)	(193)	(105)		(84)	(78)	(52)

Antony and Cleopatra   Egypt   Rome   Antony and Cleopatra   Octavius   Cleopatra   Pompey

The three short scenes which follow this opening group are, like the three castle scenes in *Macbeth,* transitional. They are identical in structure: in each a major character—Octavius, Cleopatra, Pompey—discusses Antony with a confidant. In the middle of each a messenger enters—Octavius' to bring news of Pompey, Cleopatra's with tidings from Antony, and Pompey's reporting the situation in Rome. This second group continues the idleness-activity motif, the two energetic Roman scenes framing the central panel, in which Cleopatra, so vigorous in Antony's presence, is now shown bored and listless, yawning for a potion to sleep out the time Antony is away.

In *Macbeth,* the field and castle scenes lead to the pivotal murder scene. The seventh scene (II.ii) of *Antony and Cleopatra,* which shows the meeting between Antony and Octavius at which Antony consents to marry Octavia, is analogous in position and function. This scene, which runs 246 lines, is a diptych, showing two very different meetings juxtaposed for comparison—first Antony's reconciliation with Octavius, and then Enobarbus' relation of Antony's original meeting with Cleopatra, the famous description of Cleopatra in her barge. Roman grandeur, the stiff pride of Antony and Octavius, is balanced against gorgeous Egyptian pageantry. Roman love, the cooly contracted political marriage with virtuous Octavia, is contrasted with the rich sensuality of the queen who makes defect perfection, surpassing Venus herself in amorous beauty. Like the murder in *Macbeth,* this scene divides the initial movement of the tragedy into two distinct phases, the first concerned with Antony's departure from Egypt and the second with the establishing of harmony between Antony and Octavius and throughout the Empire.

The first part of *Antony and Cleopatra* is highly designed according to Shakespeare's normal principles of construction. What is most notable about this play, however, is not the opening but the remainder, which, except for the central scene, reveals hardly any design at all. We do find the normal two movements here: in the initial movement Antony travels from Egypt to Rome and reaches an accommodation with Octavius; in the latter movement Octavius travels from Rome to Egypt and demolishes the lovers' world. The centerpiece and turning point is the scene which reveals that Antony has returned to Cleopatra, III.vi. In this little diptych the first panel gives us a picture—in Octavius' words—of Antony and Cleopatra enthroned in the marketplace of Alexandria; the second panel gives us the picture of Octavius in Rome as he welcomes Octavia home, assuring her that she has been grievously wronged. At 98 lines, however, this scene can hardly be called "major." Nor can we speak of it as in any sense the "heart of the mystery." The overall design of *Antony and Cleopatra* is so deemphasized and, relatively speaking, so unimportant in the effective structure of the play, that it seems almost vestigial. The effective structure is of course provided by the contrast between Egypt and Rome, established at the beginning and kept before us throughout. In no other tragedy does Shakespeare set up quite so emphatic a thematic opposition. It is the clarity and boldness of this opposition that makes it possible for him to deemphasize overall design and yet multiply scenes at a dizzying rate to achieve an epic effect. The result, however, is that in this play the "heart of the mystery" is not *located* at all, and this may be one reason why this tragedy, while surely one of Shakespeare's greatest, is also one of his most elusive and ambiguous plays.

The Late Romances

If *Antony and Cleopatra* had been written some years earlier, would it more nearly have resembled *Hamlet* or *Othello* in design? It is possible that the many short scenes and the deemphasized overall design are merely Shakespeare's response to the kind of material he is working with here and that the play would have been much the same, at least in these respects, whenever it was written. My own suspicion, however, is that this tragedy reflects a particular moment in Shakespeare's artistic development. Reading *Lear, Macbeth,* and *Antony and Cleopatra* in order, one gets the impression of a playwright searching for artistic freedom, a playwright feeling constrained by his own proved methods of working and looking for new techniques. About this time, Shakespeare begins to write a new kind of play, and, from the perspective of design as well as from several other points of view, *Antony and Cleopatra* can be seen as the natural bridge between the tragedies and the late romances.

Structurally, the most striking thing about both *Pericles* and *Cymbeline* is their ostentatious artlessness. *Pericles* in particular is conspicuously "naive," not only in its choice of fashionably old-fashioned Greek romance subject matter but also in its technique, a completely episodic series of short scenes, ingenuously hopping about the entire Mediterranean world. *Pericles* is not quite a burlesque of moldy tales and archaic dramatic forms, but it is close to one. Most obviously archaic is the use of Gower, the Presenter, who comments upon the narrative at every turn and introduces the old-fashioned dumb shows.

While *Cymbeline* contains nothing quite equivalent to Gower, it, too, is conspicuously loose and episodic. With the significant exception of the long and elaborate recognition scene finale, Shakespeare seems almost purposely to be avoiding design either in individual scenes or in the play as a whole. We find no central scene and only vestiges of the normal two-movement pattern when, in approximately the middle of the play, Belarius and his "sons" are introduced and the center of action shifts from the court worlds of England and Italy to the pastoral world of Wales. The entire plot of *Cymbeline* is of course highly improbable, but the curious thing is not this so much as the fact that, especially in the patterned recognition scene, the play seems to call attention to its own improbability. Just before the major recognition, for example, as Imogen steps forward to reveal her identity, Posthumus irritably pushes her away and asks, "Shall's have a play of this?" (V.v.228). A moment later, as Pisanio explains that he thought the poison he had from the queen was precious medicine, Cymbeline exclaims, "New matter still" (243).

What I am suggesting is that in both *Pericles* and *Cymbeline* the absence of overall design, the episodic structure reminiscent of such antique plays as *Clyomon and Clamydes,* is intentional and can be seen as symptomatic of a quest for technical liberty. Moreover, even as he is attempting to explore a freer dramatic form, Shakespeare's art is turning inward, turning back upon itself. The direction taken in these plays leads naturally to the two final masterpieces, *The Winter's Tale* and *The Tempest,* in both of which art itself becomes a dominant theme.⁷

One reason *Pericles* and *Cymbeline* are less successful than *The Winter's Tale* and *The Tempest* is that strategic artlessness proved self-defeating. In depriving himself of design Shakespeare deprived himself of the very art which helped to make his earlier plays so rich. After *Cymbeline* he seems to have concluded that the freedom he had been seeking was a vain illusion, that artifice is after all the soul of art. At any rate, in the last plays he turns about-face, reversing the direction in which he had been moving since *Antony and Cleopatra. Pericles* and *Cymbeline* are ostentatiously artless; *The Winter's Tale* and *The Tempest* are ostentatiously artful. Not only are these plays elaborately designed; here design seems contrived to call attention to itself.

Let us note that this—that is, design that calls attention to itself—is not an altogether new departure for Shakespeare. The conspicuous patterning of certain scenes in *Love's Labor's Lost,* for example, is possibly related to the play's theme of artifice— or, more exactly, affectation—versus naturalness. Furthermore, the conspicuous overall design of *A Midsummer Night's Dream* may, like the moonlight that filters so effectively through Shakespeare's play and so ineffectively through Bottom's, be related to this play's self-conscious concern with itself and with the nature of the poetic imagination.

I have referred frequently in the preceding chapters to *A Midsummer Night's Dream* and *The Winter's Tale* precisely because in both plays the overall design is so conspicuous. *The Winter's Tale* is a great diptych, but of course there is a brief centerpiece as well, the Chorus. Time presents himself as if he were the playwright responsible for the story. He speaks of "my scene"—that is, "my play"—and, even though this is his first and only appearance, curiously reminds us that earlier "I mentioned a son o'th'king's, which Florizel / I now name to you" (IV.i.22–23). Every word in his speech seems chosen to suggest the playwright as well as the allegorical figure:

> I, that please some, try all, both joy and terror
> Of good and bad, that makes and unfolds error,
> Now take upon me, in the name of Time,
> To use my wings. Impute it not a crime
> To me or my swift passage that I slide
> O'er sixteen years and leave the growth untried
> Of that wide gap, since it is in my power
> To o'erthrow law and in one self-born hour
> To plant and o'erwhelm custom.   (1–9)

It is tempting to speculate that perhaps Shakespeare himself delivered this speech, reminding an audience familiar with the unities of his power to overthrow rules, to do what he pleases so long as his purpose is worthy. More to the point, however, is the Chorus' structural function.

The Winter's Tale, as most interpreters agree, is concerned with the relationship between art and nature, a theme expounded in the Polixenes-Perdita debate about gillyvors. Polixenes asks why Perdita spurns these streaked flowers:

> *Perdita.*   For I have heard it said
>   There is an art which in their piedness shares
>   With great creating nature.
> *Polixenes.*   Say there be;
>   Yet nature is made better by no mean
>   But nature makes that mean. So, over that art
>   Which you say adds to nature, is an art
>   That nature makes. You see, sweet maid, we marry
>   A gentler scion to the wildest stock,
>   And make conceive a bark of baser kind
>   By bud of nobler race. This is an art
>   Which does mend nature—change it rather—but
>   The art itself is nature.   (IV.iv.86–97)

Through Paulina's art and Camillo's, their visions of what might be and their manipulation of the royal characters to achieve their visions, fallen nature is "mended" and the happy ending reached. Yet in the course of the play the distinction between the natural and the artificial, the pure pastoral world and the corrupt court world, becomes more and more problematic as the simple shepherdess turns out to be a princess and a tale of marvels so unlikely that it sounds like an old ballad turns out to be true. The final dramatic realization of the art-nature theme, the demonstration of how art in harmony with nature can repair the ruins of the fall and of how art and nature are ultimately indistinguishable, is of course the statue that comes alive when Leontes awakes his faith. The figure of Time in the center of the play, the image of an artificer who is also a force of nature, is thus an emblem of the play's central concern, and, if we take the sentiment behind *The Winter's Tale* seriously, we can perhaps understand why Shakespeare ascribes to "great creating nature" the authorship of one of his most plainly artificial plays.

The Winter's Tale celebrates the triumph of art; *The Tempest* is concerned with its limitations. The central theme is discipline, restraint, the hard labor through which one earns freedom. The two inhuman characters, Caliban and Ariel, conceived in a mode not quite allegorical but close to it, define the theme's opposite poles. So long as he is intractable, uneducable, the earthy monster Caliban will remain a slave. Ariel, too, is a slave, but of a different quality, and overarching *The Tempest* rainbowlike is the story of Ariel laboring hard for the freedom that Prospero grants him in the play's final line. Prospero's own story relates to the same theme. In Milan he indulged himself in his magical studies to the exclusion of his princely responsibilities, with the result that he lost his dukedom and found himself exiled to the enchanted island. On the island he has learned to govern a new little commonwealth, restraining Caliban and employing Ariel usefully. Equally important, he has learned to use his magic, his art, not merely for his own delight but for a purpose, to help mend the natures of his former enemies—or, in the language of this play, to help them find themselves—and in the process to earn his own freedom. Throughout the play, even as he demands discipline from others, Prospero shows the strictest self-control, in particular restraining his impulse to revenge, choosing the rarer action instead. The ultimate mark of his self-control, and self-knowledge, is his lenten renunciation of the art that has both imprisoned and freed him, his vow to break his staff and drown his book.

Curiously enough, *The Tempest* has sometimes been seen as one of Shakespeare's more self-indulgent plays. We recall Bradley's remark about Prospero's long expository speech to Miranda in the second scene, that "Shakespeare grew at last rather negligent of technique."[8] Actually, this episode is an emblematic statement of the play's theme. Prospero is educating his daughter, teaching her what she is, and the reason the episode seemed awkward to Bradley is that Shakespeare has contrived it to emphasize the effort self-knowledge requires, for Prospero is continually interrupting himself to demand that his pupil pay attention. So far from being sloppy in technique, *The Tempest* is one of the most disciplined, most severely controlled plays in the canon. In *The Winter's Tale* Shakespeare insisted upon poetic freedom, his right to overthrow law and slide past sixteen years in a moment. Here he just as ostentatiously obeys the unities, obeys them so strictly in fact that at the end of the play Alonso can point out that it is just three hours since he and his son were shipwrecked.

The play's design is also conspicuously disciplined. There are only nine scenes in all, the fewest in any play since *A Midsummer Night's Dream:* no longer is Shakespeare allowing himself the freedom of many short scenes. The central scene is the fifth (III.i), which provides the crucial emblematic tableau, the picture of Ferdinand joyfully carrying logs, laboring to win Miranda, while Prospero, who has set the task to discipline the youth "lest too light winning / Make the prize light" (I.ii.452–453), looks benevolently on unseen.

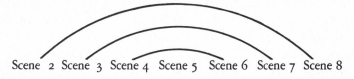

Scene 2	Scene 3	Scene 4	Scene 5	Scene 6	Scene 7	Scene 8
Prosp.,	Alonso,	Caliban,	Ferd.	Caliban,	Alonso,	Prosp.,
Ferd.,	Sebas.,	Steph.,	and	Steph.,	Sebas.,	Ferd.,
Miranda	Anton.	Trinc.	Miranda	Trinc.	Anton.	Miranda

The scene immediately preceding the centerpiece, the fourth (II.ii), is concerned with Caliban, Stephano, and Trinculo, the base characters; so is the sixth (III.ii), the one immediately following the centerpiece. The third scene (II.i) is concerned with Alonso, Sebastian, Antonio, and the other court characters; so is the seventh (III.iii), the corresponding scene on the opposite side of the centerpiece. The last segment of the second scene (I.ii), like the centerpiece, is concerned with Prospero, Ferdinand, and Miranda; so is the first segment of the eighth (IV.i). Surrounding the centerpiece, and accounting for almost the entire play, is thus an extraordinary triple frame comprised of distinct character groups.[9]

Unlike the symmetrical design of *The Winter's Tale,* the elaborate patterning of *The Tempest* has little dramatic function. Together with the obedience to the unities it seems to be merely a display of virtuosity, a pyrotechnical grand finale from the age's most accomplished dramatist on the eve of his retirement. Alternatively, both the unities and the design can be regarded as the structural correlative to the central theme—discipline. Like Prospero, Shakespeare derives the authority to preach self-control from his own practice.

If *The Tempest* is in some ways Shakespeare's most self-assertive play, the one in which he actually seems to flaunt his own accomplishments, it is also perhaps his most modest. Nearly everyone has noticed Prospero's somewhat contemptuous attitude toward his rough magic. "I must / Bestow upon the eyes of this young couple / Some vanity of mine art," he says as he prepares to stage the Ceres masque; "it is my promise, / And they expect it of me" (IV.i.39–42). Art in this play is seen as an insubstantial pageant, a beautiful but baseless vision like the banquet that Ariel conjures for Alonso or like Prospero's betrothal-gift masque. Like the banquet and the masque, and like the great globe itself—Shakespeare's Globe as well as the earth—the bright dream of art is seen as something fundamentally not to be trusted: inevitably the dream must dissolve, leaving us in the dimmer world of such as Antonio and Caliban—that thing of darkness that Prospero acknowledges as his own. Because it is in a sense unreal, the dream world of art, so laboriously achieved over so many years of discipline, is itself a kind of prison and life in it a kind of exile. Shakespeare's last major play does not end—like the masque, it dissolves, as Prospero, possibly played by Shakespeare, steps forward, delicately reminds the audience of their own failings, and begs to be set free from his enchanted island.

At the conclusion of his career, then, Shakespeare's art turns inward and feeds upon itself. In *The Winter's Tale* and *The Tempest* the principles of design, which have all along been one of Shakespeare's chief technical resources, become something more, as, in the final romances, the methods of his art become the subject as well.

Notes

Index

Notes

Chapter 1: Contexts of Design

1. *Themes and Conventions of Elizabethan Tragedy* (Cambridge: Cambridge University Press, 1935), p. 5.

2. *Endeavors of Art: A Study of Form in Elizabethan Drama* (Madison: University of Wisconsin Press, 1954). Building upon Miss Doran's work, Bernard Beckerman infuses her ideas with his own understanding of Elizabethan theatrical conditions and his feeling for the emotional rhythms of drama. See *Shakespeare at the Globe* and *Dynamics of Drama: Theory and Method of Analysis* (New York: Alfred A. Knopf, 1970). For a recent study concerned with a special aspect of multiple unity see Richard Levin, *The Multiple Plot in English Renaissance Drama* (Chicago: University of Chicago Press, 1971).

3. See especially Alfred Harbage, *Shakespeare and the Rival Traditions* (New York: Macmillan, 1952); Bernard Spivack, *Shakespeare and the Allegory of Evil* (New York: Columbia University Press, 1958); David M. Bevington, *From Mankind to Marlowe* (Cambridge, Mass.: Harvard University Press, 1962); R. G. Hunter, *Shakespeare and the Comedy of Forgiveness* (New York: Columbia University Press, 1965); and Glynne Wickham, *Shakespeare's Dramatic Heritage* (London: Routledge & Kegan Paul, 1969).

4. *Shakespearean Tragedy*, 2nd ed. (London: Macmillan, 1905), p. 72.

5. "Mirror-Scenes in Shakespeare," in *Joseph Quincy Adams Memorial Studies*, ed. J. G. McManaway et al. (Washington, D.C.: Folger Shakespeare Library, 1948), pp. 101–113. Paul J. Aldus develops a similar train of thought in "Analogical Probability in Shakespeare's Plays," *Shakespeare Quarterly*, 6 (1955), 397–414.

6. *Construction in Shakespeare*, University of Michigan Contributions in Modern Philology, 17 (Ann Arbor: University of Michigan Press, 1951), p. 26.

7. "The Jacobean Shakespeare: Some Observations on the Construction of the Tragedies," in *Jacobean Theatre*, ed. John Russell Brown and Bernard Harris, Stratford-upon-Avon Studies, 1 (London: Edward Arnold, 1960), pp. 11–41.

8. On the emblem books in general see Mario Praz, *Studies in Seventeenth-Century Imagery*, 2 vols. (London: the Warburg Institute, 1939–1947), and Rosemary Freeman, *English Emblem Books* (London: Chatto & Windus, 1948). In connection with Shakespeare and the Elizabethan drama,

Henry Green's *Shakespeare and the Emblem Writers* (London, 1870) is now outdated, but see Dieter Mehl, "Emblems in English Renaissance Drama," in *Renaissance Drama*, ed. S. Schoenbaum, new series II (Evanston, Ill.: Northwestern University Press, 1969), 39-57.

9. On the fusing of painting and poetry in the Renaissance see Rensselaer W. Lee, *Ut Pictura Poesis: The Humanistic Theory of Painting* (New York: W. W. Norton, 1967), and Jean Hagstrum, *The Sister Arts* (Chicago: University of Chicago Press, 1958). Dryden's "A Parallel of Poetry and Painting" is a compendium of Renaissance commonplaces on the subject.

10. *Shakespeare at the Globe*, pp. 24-62.

11. George Kernodle, talking about the close relationship between Elizabethan drama and street tableaux, notes the frequency of episodes in which "the choice of material was determined by the habit of picking for illustrative art and street art a static situation that would catch the eye and hold it for a full lyric realization of the emotion" (*From Art to Theatre: Form and Convention in the Renaissance*, Chicago: University of Chicago Press, 1944, p. 147). On tableaux in Shakespeare and the general relationship between Elizabethan stagecraft and the visual arts, see also W. Moelwyn Merchant, *Shakespeare and the Artist* (London: Oxford University Press, 1959), especially ch. i. The *tableaux vivants* of the annual Lord Mayor's shows and royal progresses provide clues to the same aspect of the Renaissance sensibility as the emblem books. Glynne Wickham, developing Kernodle's pioneering work, studies their relationship to English theatrical tradition in *Early English Stages*, 2 vols. to date (London: Routledge & Kegan Paul, 1963—). See also David M. Bergeron's account of the development of the Lord Mayor's shows and royal progresses, *English Civic Pageantry 1558-1642* ·(London: Edward Arnold, 1971).

12. See E. H. Gombrich, "Moment and Movement in Art," *Journal of the Warburg and Courtauld Institutes*, 27 (1964), 293-306.

13. See M. H. Abrams, *The Mirror and the Lamp* (Oxford: Oxford University Press, 1953), pp. 50-51, and, for a slightly different view, Jean Hagstrum, "The Sister Arts: From Neoclassic to Romantic," *Comparatists at Work*, ed. Stephen G. Nichols, Jr., and Richard B. Vowles (Waltham, Mass.: Blaisdell, 1968), pp. 169-194.

14. See Walter J. Ong, S.J., "From Allegory to Diagram in the Renaissance Mind: A Study in the Significance of the Allegorical Tableau," *The Journal of Aesthetics & Art Criticism*, 17 (1959), 423-440, and the same author's "System, Space, and Intellect in Renaissance Symbolism," *The Barbarian Within* (New York: Macmillan, 1962), pp. 68-87. Most of the work on spatial form in poetry has been done in connection with number symbolism, a controversial subject among Renaissance specialists. Of course one does not have to agree with particular interpretations the numerologists have put forward in order to accept their larger argument that the Renaissance thought of poetic form in spatial terms. See especially Alastair Fowler, *Triumphal Forms: Structural Patterns in Eliza-*

bethan Poetry (Cambridge: Cambridge University Press, 1970), and Christopher Butler, *Number Symbolism* (London: Routledge & Kegan Paul, 1970). In "Spatial Form in Modern Literature," *The Widening Gyre* (New Brunswick, N.J.: Rutgers University Press, 1963), pp. 3–62, Joseph Frank suggests that such writers as Eliot, Pound, Proust, and Joyce are indicative of a modern renaissance of spatial form. Frank's discussion of the presentation of character in Proust should be compared with my own brief comments on the subject in Shakespeare.

15. "Poetry and Design in William Blake," *The Journal of Aesthetics & Art Criticism*, 10 (1951), 41.

16. "The Structure of Imagery in *The Faerie Queene*," *University of Toronto Quarterly*, 30 (1961), 109–110.

17. See Thomas P. Roche, Jr., *The Kindly Flame: A Study of the Third and Fourth Books of Spenser's Faerie Queene* (Princeton, N.J.: Princeton University Press, 1964), pp. 195–211, and Fowler, *Triumphal Forms*, pp. 108–112.

18. See Nelson, *The Poetry of Edmund Spenser* (New York: Columbia University Press, 1963), pp. 93–96. For Hieatt's numerological analysis see *Short Time's Endless Monument* (New York: Columbia University Press, 1960).

19. See Brooks Otis, *Virgil: A Study in Civilized Poetry* (Oxford: Clarendon Press, 1963), and the same author's *Ovid as an Epic Poet*, 2nd ed. (Cambridge: Cambridge University Press, 1970). In *Homer and the Heroic Tradition* (Cambridge, Mass.: Harvard University Press, 1958), Cedric H. Whitman proposes an elaborate symmetrical design for the *Iliad*.

20. Professor Martz' discussion of *Hero and Leander* will appear in his facsimile of the unique copy of the first edition to be published by the Folger Shakespeare Library. I am grateful to him for allowing me to use a photocopy of his introduction.

21. For a general discussion of patterns of central emphasis in Elizabethan poetry see Fowler, *Triumphal Forms*, chs. ii–v. Fowler's suggestion that centralized motifs in the arts and political ceremony derive from the "iconology of cosmic kingship" (p. 23) seems unconvincing. Structural patterns f this kind have a history—that is, the variations on the patterns can be traced—but do they necessarily have an "origin"? It appears more likely that when form is conceived spatially the importance of the central position follows perforce. Perhaps instead of seeking an historical "source" for central emphasis it would be more valuable to consider the problem from the perspective of psychology and epistemology.

22. Heinrich Wölfflin's *Principles of Art History*, tr. M. D. Hoffinger (London: G. Bell, 1932), originally published in 1915, is still the classic discussion of balanced design in Renaissance art.

23. Kernodle's thesis in *From Art to Theatre* is that there is a line of descent from the ancient theater screen through medieval and Renaissance art and the *tableax vivants* to the spatial organization of the variou Renaissance theaters, including the Elizabethan theater. In the cour

of his argument Kernodle provides a history of the pattern of design I am describing. The precise nature and function of the "discovery space" or "inner stage" or "booth" is disputed, but its existence and use for tableaux is not. On the composition of symmetrical stage pictures see Beckerman, *Shakespeare at the Globe*, pp. 165–176.

24. *De re aedificatoria*, ix, 5; ed. Giovanni Orlandi, 2 vols. (Milan: Edizioni Il Polefilio, 1966). I have appropriated Sir Anthony Blunt's translation of this passage from *Artistic Theory in Italy 1450–1600* (Oxford: Clarendon Press, 1940), p. 15. On the general subject of proportion see Erwin Panofsky, "The History of the Theory of Human Proportions as a Reflection of the History of Styles," in *Meaning in the Visual Arts* (Garden City, N.Y.: Doubleday Anchor Books, 1955), pp. 55–107; Rudolf Wittkower, *Architectural Principles in the Age of Humanism* (London: the Warburg Institute, 1949); and P. H. Scholfield, *The Theory of Proportion in Architecture* (Cambridge: Cambridge University Press, 1958). This aspect of Renaissance aesthetic theory has recently been discussed in connection with number symbolism in poetry; see Butler, *Number Symbolism*, especially ch. v.

25. Ed. Gladys Doidge Willcock and Alice Walker (Cambridge: Cambridge University Press, 1936), p. 64.

26. "The Structural Pattern of 'The Winter's Tale,' " *Review of English Literature*, 5 (1964), 72–82. See also William Blissett, "This Wide Gap of Time: *The Winter's Tale*," *English Literary Renaissance*, 1 (1971), 52–70.

27. T. W. Baldwin is the principal exponent of the five-act theory. Even if one must disagree with Baldwin's conclusions, *William Shakspere's Five-Act Structure* (Urbana: University of Illinois Press, 1947) is a fascinating history of an important critical idea. See also his *On Act and Scene Division in the Shakspere First Folio* (Carbondale: Southern Illinois University Press, 1965). Henry L. Snuggs, *Shakespeare and Five Acts: Studies in a Dramatic Convention* (New York: Vantage Press, 1960), also surveys the history of the convention, using comparative analysis of four representative plays and their sources to demonstrate that Shakespeare did not rework his sources into a five-act structure. Wilfred T. Jewkes, *Act Division in Elizabethan and Jacobean Plays 1583–1616* (Hamden, Conn.: the Shoestring Press, 1958) examines the surviving plays statistically to determine which classes of plays were divided and which were not, concluding that Shakespeare did not employ act division. I have summarized Jewkes's argument below. See also Alfred Harbage's succinct and suggestive "Shakespeare's Technique," in *The Complete Pelican Shakespeare* (Baltimore: Penguin Books, 1969), pp. 30–39.

28. "Preface to Shakespeare, *Johnson on Shakespeare*, ed. Walter Raleigh (Oxford: Oxford University Press, 1965), p. 57.

29. See Jewkes, *Act Division*, pp. 7–9.

30. See Beckerman, *Shakespeare at the Globe*, pp. 176–177, and Bevington, *Mankind to Marlowe*, p. 97.

Chapter 2: The Shakespearean Scene

1. The passage of time is marked with some precision. It is still early morning when Cornwall commands that Kent will sit in the stocks "till noon" (II.ii.129). It is later when the gentleman who arrives with Lear speaks of the "night before" (II.iv.3), but evidently before noon because Lear can still say to Cornwall and Regan, "Good morrow to you both" (II.iv.122). In the latter part of the scene, during the long quarrel between Lear and his daughters, references to time are omitted so that the compressed passage of the day from noon to evening will not seem too abrupt. Yet most readers, I find, assume that it is evening when Kent falls asleep, that Lear arrives the next morning, and that the scene as a whole covers not one but two days. Shakespeare himself introduces this ambiguity when Regan demands a longer punishment for Kent than Cornwall has ordered: "Till noon? Till night, my lord, and all night too" (II.ii.130). And before falling asleep Kent says, "Fortune, good night" (II.ii.168). This sense of day, night, and day again is reinforced by the scene's rhythm, the bustle of the first part gradually leading to the quiet of the middle section, followed by new activity when Lear arrives. What we are dealing with, in fact, is an instance in miniature of double time. The single day scheme helps unify the scene as a whole; the two day scheme helps to emphasize the analogy between the unjust treatment of Kent and Lear.

2. See T. W. Craik, *The Tudor Interlude* (Leicester: Leicester University Press, 1967), pp. 93–96.

3. *Shakespeare's Dramatic Heritage* (London: Routledge & Kegan Paul, 1969), pp. 214–224.

4. Cf. Nevil Coghill, *Shakespeare's Professional Skills* (Cambridge: Cambridge University Press, 1964), p. 62. Coghill uses this phrase from *Hamlet* to describe the relations between juxtaposed scenes.

5. *Prefaces to Shakespeare*, vol. II (Princeton, N.J.: Princeton University Press, 1947), p. 304.

6. "Shakespeare and the Stoicism of Seneca," *Selected Essays* (London: Faber and Faber, 1958), p. 130.

7. The standard study of Shakespearean rhetoric is Sister Miriam Joseph, *Shakespeare's Use of the Arts of Language* (New York: Columbia University Press, 1947), illustrated with a wealth of examples for each of the figures.

8. There is a textual problem in the central segment of this speech. Q1 (1594) prints an extra three and a half lines; evidently they are misplaced or else Shakespeare intended to cancel them. The structure of the speech is clear in the Folio text. On the rhetorical framing pattern here see Walter F. Schirmer, "Shakespeare und die Rhetorik," *Shakespeare-Jahrbuch*, 71 (1935), 11–31.

9. *Euphues: The Anatomy of Wit and Euphues & His England*, ed. Morris William Croll and Harry Clemons (London: George Routledge & Sons,

1916), p. 40. Croll's classic introductory essay discusses the origins of the euphuistic style and its relation to Elizabethan taste.

10. *Shakespeare and the Common Understanding* (New York: the Free Press, 1967), p. 12.

Chapter 3: Design in Groups of Scenes

1. For other pairs analogous in function to the lovers' scenes in *Romeo and Juliet* see the two Polonii Scenes in *Hamlet* (I.iii and IV.v), discussed in Chapter 4, or the murder and England scenes in *Macbeth*, discussed in Chapter 6.

2. Cf. Una Ellis-Fermor's discussion of the *Macbeth* episodes which Shakespeare chose not to dramatize (*Shakespeare the Dramatist*, London: Methuen, 1961, pp. 93–97).

3. Cf. Nevil Coghill's discussion of juxtaposition of scenes, *Shakespeare's Professional Skills* (Cambridge: Cambridge University Press, 1964), pp. 61–77. Coghill also discusses the opening of *Twelfth Night* and the alternation of scenes in *1 Henry IV*. His analysis of *1 Henry IV*, however, seems to imply that act divisions are significant, which I do not believe they are.

4. On *anadiplosis* see Sister Miriam Joseph, *Shakespeare's Use of the Arts of Language* (New York: Columbia University Press, 1947), pp. 82–83.

5. *Shakespeare from Richard II to Henry V* (Stanford, Calif.: Stanford University Press, 1957), pp. 62–63.

6. See Chapter 6.

7. These are the only times the stage is cleared. The traditional divisions ignore the characters sleeping onstage between II.ii and III.i, and between III.ii and IV.i. The Folio gives the direction "They sleepe all the Act" at the end of III.ii, but Q1 (1600) indicates that originally the action was continuous. A number of critics have speculated that the Folio direction may refer to a private theater performance or a revival.

8. Cf. Robert Heilman, *Magic in the Web: Action and Language in "Othello"* (Lexington: University of Kentucky Press, 1956), p. 170: "The spatial form of Act I gives a clue to Shakespeare's way of perceiving the love theme. The act not only begins but also ends with Iago's openly stating his hatred and translating it into schemes against Othello." After pointing out parallels between the two segments Heilman remarks, "So Iago has both ends of Act I; thus his actions symbolically hem in or surround those of Othello and Desdemona, whose love is first dramatized in the middle of the act." In *Shakespeare and the Allegory of Evil* (New York: Columbia University Press, 1958), Bernard Spivack has demonstrated that Iago is descended from the morality Vice. It is interesting to note in this connection that the Vice in the older drama is often used as a framing character, symbolically surrounding the protagonist. See, for instance, the final scene of *Cambises* in which Ambidexter's soliloquies frame the tyrant's death.

9. The Folio makes no mention of lights in I.iii, but the Q1 (1622) stage direction which calls for a table, lights, and attendants has been widely adopted. My discussion has been influenced by Alvin Kernan's excellent introduction to his Signet edition of *Othello* (New York: New American Library, 1963) and by Norman Rabkin's interpretation, *Shakespeare and the Common Understanding*, (New York: the Free Press, 1967), pp. 57–73.

10. A word about "scenes" and "groups." It does not help our understanding of Shakespearean structure if we insist upon too rigid a definition of "scene" or too rigorous a distinction between "scenes" and "groups." The Battle of Towton sequence from *3 Henry VI*, for instance, which I discussed earlier as a "scene," might alternatively be considered a "group," and there are a number of other borderline cases, including of course all the battle sequences. For example, *Winter's Tale* IV.iv, the pastoral episode in which Polixenes attends the shepherds' festival and attempts to break up the match between Florizel and Perdita, is one of the longest scenes in Shakespeare—only the finale of *Love's Labor's Lost* is longer. For over 800 lines the action proceeds without a cleared stage. Shakespeare's typical structural pattern emerges, however, only when the long festival scene is considered in connection with the much shorter preceding one, but then the lucid architecture is unmistakable. Autolycus is introduced in IV.iii as a kind of mischievous cuckoo in human form, who ushers in the new spring-like mood of the play as he enters singing "When daffodils begin to peer." The body of the scene is given to the amusing episode in which Autolycus cozens the rustic clown, an episode which finds its counterpart in the final segment of the festival scene when he once again cozens the clown, this time together with the old shepherd, his father. In the first episode Autolycus' purpose is simply fun and profit; in the second, however, the very spirit of spring has been caught up in the mysterious forces moving the play toward a happy ending, and Autolycus prevents the rustics from going to Polixenes, sending them instead to Florizel on the seashore. The two cozening episodes frame the long pastoral centerpiece, marking off a distinct unit. But what shall we call this unit? Obviously Shakespeare would never have given a moment's thought to the question. His interest was merely in shaping dramatic material into expressive patterns, and generally we will have no trouble perceiving his designs if we do not allow terminology to get in our way.

Chapter 4: The Design of Hamlet

1. See Maynard Mack's classic essay "The World of *Hamlet*," *Yale Review*, 41 (1952), 502–523. Some of the ideas that appear in this chapter are presented in different form in my "*Hamlet* and the Shape of Revenge," *English Literary Renaissance*, I (1971), 132–143, in which I focus on the theatrical metaphor. J. K. Walton also analyzes the play scene by scene in "The Structure of *Hamlet*," *Hamlet*, ed. John Russell Brown

and Bernard Harris, Stratford-upon-Avon Studies, 5 (London: Edward Arnold, 1963), pp. 44–89. Stephen Booth suggests an interesting approach to structure based on the playwright's manipulation of his audience in "On the Value of *Hamlet*," *Reinterpretations of Elizabethan Drama*, ed. Norman Rabkin (New York: Columbia University Press, 1969), pp. 137–176.

2. The improper division of the fourth scene is the work of the eighteenth-century editors. There is a momentarily cleared stage but no change in time or place, and the action is plainly continuous. See Granville-Barker, *Prefaces to Shakespeare*, vol. I (Princeton, N.J.: Princeton University Press, 1946), p. 57, who argues against the division. In this case as in one other, scene 10, Willard Farnham's Pelican edition follows tradition and divides improperly.

3. "Shakespeare's Technique," in *The Complete Pelican Shakespeare* (Baltimore: Penguin Books, 1969), p. 32.

4. This scene is usually divided improperly, I believe, by editors who reconstruct the action from the Q2 (1604–1605) directions. Q2 marks no exit for the queen after her conversation with Hamlet, but does mark an entrance for her with the king and Rosencrantz and Guildenstern. This would mean that she must exit and reenter immediately or after a short pause. But a punctuating pause is not called for at this point, as it is, for example, after the mousetrap scene. The Folio directions seem more logical than those of Q2. The Folio clearly indicates that the queen remains onstage while Hamlet exits with Polonius' body. Probably she stands sighing and wringing her hands until Claudius enters and comments on her distraction: "There's matter in these sighs. These profound heaves / You must translate; 'tis fit we understand them" (IV.i.1–2). This speech, perfectly understandable if the Folio directions are followed, becomes awkward and even somewhat obscure if the queen is supposed to exit. Q1 (1603), the bad quarto, supports the Folio directions.

5. *Shakespearean Tragedy*, 2nd ed. (London: Macmillan, 1905), pp. 59–60. Bradley remarks that similar reappearances occur after the crisis in *Julius Caesar*, *Macbeth*, and *Antony and Cleopatra*.

Chapter 5: The Early Plays

1. Examination of design suggests limitations in the critical position of those who would sentimentalize Shylock, turning *The Merchant of Venice* into "The Tragedy of the Jew." Structurally, *The Merchant of Venice* is a romantic comedy with the Bassanio-Portia love story as the main plot and the Antonio-Shylock story as the subplot. The central scene is not the trial, but Bassanio's casket choice (III.ii), which comes in the actual center of the play. This long scene is concerned with the play's first dominant theme, hazard or risk, the theme which unites main plot and subplot. Just as Antonio daily risks his substance in his commercial ventures—unlike Shylock, who profits without risk—so

here Bassanio is shown hazarding his life for love. By selecting the lead casket, demonstrating that he is not deceived by superficial glitter, Bassanio proves his worth and his right to marry Portia. His triumph is the emblematic core of the love story and the turning point in his "venture." The turning point in Antonio's analogous venture—that is, the pivot of the subplot—comes in the same scene. No sooner has Bassanio won his love than a messenger reports that Antonio's vessels have foundered and his bond is forfeit. After this pivotal scene the play's concerns change as the risk theme yields to the new dominant theme of mercy, the triumph of mercy over justice in the trial prefiguring the analogous triumph in the main plot finale when Portia and Nerissa forgive Bassanio and Gratiano for parting with their rings. Some critics and most directors, however, have problems with the symbolic casket scene. On the stage it is often played for laughs and the trial made the climax and turning point of the play. But, great theater though it is, the trial is only the finale of the Antonio-Shylock subplot, and when it receives disproportionate emphasis the overall design is obscured and the main plot finale at Belmont inevitably seems weak.

2. *1 Henry VI*, Arden edition, (London: Methuen, 1957), p. iii. Hereward Price uses *1 Henry VI* as his principal example of Shakespeare's constructive powers in *Construction in Shakespeare*, University of Michigan Contributions in Modern Philology, 17 (Ann Arbor: University of Michigan Press, 1951).

3. For further discussion of the "Samson pattern" and other repeated motifs see A. C. Hamilton's excellent analysis, *The Early Shakespeare* (San Marino, Calif.: the Huntington Library, 1967), pp. 9–31.

4. E. M. W. Tillyard notes that it is preeminently as a fine piece of construction that *2 Henry VI* can be enjoyed. Tillyard, however, places the turning point in the relatively minor scene (II.ii) in which York wins the Nevils to his side (*Shakespeare's History Plays*, London: Chatto and Windus, 1944, pp. 173–188). The design of the play supports J. P. Brockbrank's analysis in "The Frame of Disorder—'Henry VI,'" *Early Shakespeare*, ed. John Russell Brown and Bernard Harris, Stratford-upon-Avon Studies, 3 (London: Edward Arnold, 1961), pp. 73–99. Brockbank remarks that "the unique form of the play is yielded by the martyrdom of Gloster. The play climbs to one crisis—a central point in the third act where the killing of Gloster calls out the strongest statement of the moral-political positives; and it falls to a second—where the battle of St. Albans occasions the most powerful poetry of negation."

5. The two movements reveal many other correspondences, for example, the repeated pattern of first a son and then a father murdered—Rutland and York in the first half, the prince and King Henry in the second. See Hamilton, in *Early Shakespeare*, pp. 47–62. Most critics regard this play as relatively shapeless. Tillyard, for instance, remarks that "formlessness of a sort" was necessary to Shakespeare's purposes in portraying chaos (*Shakespeare's History Plays*, p. 190

6. The Folio omits 18 lines that appear in Q1 (597), where this

segment runs 40 lines. Even though the two movements of *Richard III* are of unequal length, Shakespeare employs the usual technique of repeated motifs to give a sense of a new beginning after the turning point. Thus old Queen Margaret, whose ritualistic laments serve as a kind of chorus, appears once in each movement (I.iii and IV.iv). The wooing scene in which Richard persuades Anne to marry him (I.ii) is balanced by a second virtuoso performance in which he persuades Queen Elizabeth to allow him to woo her daughter (IV.iv). The effect of the repeated motifs here is perhaps to emphasize the futility of Richard's attempt to prevent fortune's wheel from turning.

7. Eliot, "Seneca in Elizabethan Translation," *Selected Essays* (London: Faber and Faber, 1958), p. 82. Henslowe records "Titus & Ondronicous" as a new play when presented by Sussex's men on January 24, 1594, but many scholars, considering the tragedy crude, argue for an earlier date.

8. Perhaps the unusually short finale—V.vi runs only 52 lines—helps explain the relative brevity of the latter movement of *Richard II*. It would not be surprising to learn that the original finale was much longer and that Shakespeare condensed it for any of a number of possible reasons after deciding to continue the chronicle in the *Henry IV* plays.

9. *As You Like It* is a good example of how the two movements of a Shakespearean play usually differ in theme. The central scene, III.ii, is the one in which Rosalind and Orlando first meet in the forest. At 408 lines this is by far the longest scene in the play, and it spans the actual center. Before III.ii the dominant theme is unnaturalness, "unkind" behavior, and in this movement the romantic story tends to be suppressed. Shakespeare establishes that Rosalind and Orlando are in love and then more or less drops the subject. After falling in love in the second scene, Orlando forgets Rosalind until the central scene. Rosalind is almost equally forgetful: learning she is banished, for instance, elicits not a word about the cruelty of separation from Orlando. In the latter movement nearly every scene is a wooing episode of one sort or another. Here the parallel stories of the "unkind" brothers, Oliver and Frederick, are suppressed. Shakespeare dramatizes neither Oliver's nor Frederick's transformation, concentrating instead on showing us a little anatomy of love, the thematically connected stories of Orlando and Rosalind, Silvius and Phebe, and Touchstone and Audrey, leading to the final pageant in which Hymen appears and all join hands.

Initial movement:	Central	Latter movement:
Unnaturalness	scene	Love
(1113)	(408)	(1115)

Analysis of the central scene would show how it is organized to provide a smooth modulation from the unnaturalness to the love theme.

10. For the text of Brooke's poem and a good discussion of Shakespeare's use of his source see Geoffrey Bullough, *Narrative and Dramatic Sources of Shakespeare* vol. I (London: Routledge & Kegan Paul, 1964), pp. 269–363. Henry T Snuggs analyzes the narrative sequence in Brooke

and Shakespeare to prove that Shakespeare did not rework the poem into a five-act play. Snuggs concludes that in structure the poem and the play are almost identical (*Shakespeare and Five Acts*, New York: Vantage Press, 1960, pp. 90–111).

Chapter 6: The Later Plays

1. See Paul Aldus, "Analogical Probability," *Shakespeare Quarterly*, 6, 401, who discusses the scene in detail.

2. Cf. Norman Rabkin, *Shakespeare and the Common Understanding* (New York: the Free Press, 1967), p. 48: "If the play's structure is not a matter of conscious design, one must marvel at the intuitive genius which arranges that, immediately after the climactic exposition of the theme of the relation of time to value in the main plot, that theme should be dramatized with equal emphasis in the subplot. Thematically, III.ii and III.iii, one in the main plot, the other in the subplot, are the crucial scenes of the entire play."

3. *Shakespearean Tragedy*, 2nd ed. (London: Macmillan, 1905), p. 55.

4. The Folio makes cuts in the prologue (III.i) and the third Lear panel (III.vi), but the general proportions of the group are retained. On the organization of this sequence cf. George R. Kernodle, "The Symphonic Form of King Lear," in *Elizabethan Studies and Other Essays in Honor of George F. Reynolds* (Boulder: University of Colorado Press, 1945), pp. 185–191.

5. The arrangement of the witches' scenes is especially interesting. *Macbeth* opens with a witches' "prologue," followed by the expository scene in which Duncan hears of his generals' victories, and then the scene in which Macbeth meets the witches. The latter movement repeats the pattern, again opening with a witches' "prologue," followed by the expository scene in which the unnamed lord describes Macduff's flight, and then Macbeth's second meeting with the witches.

Initial movement			Latter movement		
I.i	I.ii	I.iii	III.v	III.vi	IV.i
Prologue: witches alone (12)	Expository scene (67)	Macbeth and witches (156)	Prologue: witches alone (36)	Expository scene (49)	Macbeth and witches (156)

Most scholars believe that III.v, the "Hecate scene," is an interpolation, possibly written by Middleton, and the arguments in favor of an interpolator are convincing. But if there was an interpolator he evidently understood Shakespeare's principles of construction, for he inserted his Hecate scene at the one point in the play where it would reinforce and not disrupt the overall design. For a summary of the major issues see Kenneth Muir's Arden edition (London: Methuen, 1951), pp. xxxv–xxxviii. In *Shakespeare's Occasional Plays* (New York: Barnes and Noble, 1965), pp. 24–31, J. M. Nosworthy argues that the interpolator is

Shakespeare himself. In his Arden edition, Muir conjectures that the second movement originally began with IV.i, Macbeth's interview with the witches, followed by the scene which now precedes it, the conversation between Lennox and the lord. If we assume an interpolator we must also omit a few lines in IV.i, but these do not affect the overall design.

6. The effect of this scene should be compared with that of the *Macbeth* murder scene in which the centerpiece, the porter, provides a comic perspective that complements the tragic side panels. It may be helpful to think of these scenes as analogous in some respects to certain Renaissance "perspectivist" paintings, for example, Holbein's *Ambassadors*. In the center of the painting, placed exactly between the two young and vigorous gentlemen, is an elongated gray smear, which, when the painting is viewed from the side, resolves itself into a death's head. Like Shakespeare's scenes, the painting makes its point by forcing us to consider its subject from two points of view. Shakespeare refers to paintings of this kind in *Richard II*, when Bushy speaks of "perspectives, which rightly gazed upon, / Show nothing but confusion—eyed awry, / Distinguish form" (II.ii.18–20). Whether Shakespeare actually tried to achieve effects analogous to those of perspectivist painting is of course impossible to say, but the relationship between his art and formal perspective in Renaissance painting might be a fruitful subject for study.

7. Cf. Rabkin, *Shakespeare and the Common Understanding*, pp. 192–237. Rabkin's analysis of the late romances takes its point of departure from Granville-Barker's insight that much of what strikes us as awkward and naive in *Cymbeline* is in fact extremely sophisticated, the play being designed to call attention to its own artlessness.

8. *Shakespearean Tragedy*, p. 42.

9. I am indebted to Michael Holahan for calling this pattern to my attention.

Index